Book endorsements

"Wow! What can I say, I highly recommend Stephanie Aldrich's *There's No Crying in the Man's World*. Her book takes a good look at the rules in the business world and how we as women fit into those rules. It takes, drive, discipline, and dedication no matter how old you are. Her approach works in a way that is positive, proactive, and professional. Set your goals high! It takes vision for you as a leader to build a culture that will lead you to success. People lead people. Be prepared and organized and surround yourself with positive, successful people that have had great successes! Ask them to help mentor you. This book provides just the insight every woman needs who enters in the business world."

Graceanne Nicholson—Regional Vice President of Operations—Sterling Jewelers Inc.

"I knew I was a successful businesswoman, but after reading Dr. Aldrich's book, I now know what it takes to become a truly powerful modern woman and compete with the big boys! Dr. Aldrich has helped me become more confident about my future and has given me the tools I will need to get there! I was especially inspired by the interviews Dr.

Aldrich did with successful women. I know if I emulate their qualities, I can achieve everything I dream!"

Katherine Raymond, DDS

"Dr. Stephanie Aldrich courageously bares her soul, frequently offering examples in her own life exposing her weaknesses, and in so doing, her strengths. Her fresh and youthful style of faith in the reader and her conviction that the high goal is attainable; Dr. Aldrich takes the reader step by step up the ladder to become the successful, powerful, modern woman in a man's world."

Alba Cook, retired Secondary Education—English

"I loved this book! Every working woman will relate to its wise and witty voice."

Diana Greenspan, Pre-Need Counselor for Funeral Homes

THERE'S NO CRYING IN THE MAN'S WORLD

THERE'S NO CRYING IN THE MAN'S WORLD

A Woman's Guide to Succeeding in Business

Dr. Stephanie Aldrich

Power Source Media, LLC

iUniverse, Inc.
New York Lincoln Shanghai

THERE'S NO CRYING IN THE MAN'S WORLD
A Woman's Guide to Succeeding in Business

iUniverse books may be ordered through booksellers or by contacting:

iUniverse
2021 Pine Lake Road, Suite 100
Lincoln, NE 68512
www.iuniverse.com
1-800-Authors (1-800-288-4677)

Because of the dynamic nature of the Internet, any Web addresses or links contained in this book may have changed since publication and may no longer be valid.

ISBN: 978-0-595-43341-4 (pbk)
ISBN: 978-0-595-87667-9 (ebk)

Printed in the United States of America

This book is dedicated to my family—Mom, Dad, and Heather who helped make me the powerful modern woman that I am today. Without your support and encouragement, I know I wouldn't have come as far as I have. Thank you, and I love you!

This book is also dedicated to all of my girls—Stacey, Becky, Kim S, Corri, Deanna, Sarah, Christine, Della, Lara, Amity, Amanda, Jen, Kim K, Leslie, Sylvia, Lori, Dawn P, and Dawn G—who live the American dream as powerful modern women. You inspire me and push me to my limits everyday! Thank you! Chi love.

Contents

Preface

Women's liberation has been going on for hundreds of years. Little by little, generation by generation women's roles in this world are changing. In the new millennium, some women have the rights and privileges of their male counterparts, and many others do not.

I am one of the luckiest women on the planet. I have been given opportunities that most women have not. I have graduated from one college and one major university with bachelor's and doctorate degrees. I have a beautiful house. I run my own million-dollar business that I started from the ground up. I have many friends who think I'm one of the funniest people they've ever met. I like to travel and have had many wonderful trips to different countries. I have a family who adores me and is very proud of the kind of woman that I've become. And I've met a man who has literally taken me to a higher level of love and maturity than I've ever known before. I am the "American Dream!"

I wrote this book for two reasons:
1. To connect with other powerful modern women.
2. To help other women become powerful modern women.

> *"It only takes one drop of water to start a flood. I want this book to start the flood and I want you to keep it going."*
>
> —Stephanie Aldrich

Acknowledgments

I want to pay tribute to the people that have gone before me in the information industry who have inspired me to write down my experiences in both dentistry and business. Mr. Jack Canfield and Mr. Mark Victor Hansen showed me how to collect my thoughts and transfer them into a book. Ms. Janet Switzer showed me how to start an information business. Mr. Dan Kennedy and Mr. Ed O'Keefe showed me how to direct market not only my dental practice but also my information business. And finally, Mr. Paul Hartunian showed me how to get as much free publicity for my businesses as humanly possible.

Thank you for your hard work and for sharing your success and roadmap with the rest of us. If it weren't for you, this book and future projects would not be possible. I've only met two of you personally, but I want to let you know that you've inspired me and my creative side to reach for things that I've never known were possible.

I want to also thank all of the women that I interviewed—Peggy, Kathy, Becky, Sharon, Gretchen, Stacey, Amanda, and Della.

I also want to thank the people at IUniverse whose guidance and wisdom made this book possible. Thank you Brenda Kluck.

Chapter 1

The Powerful Modern Woman

Women of all ages have dreams in life. We want to be healthy. We want to find someone to love. We want to find happiness. We want our spouse to have money. But in reality, half of us will end up in a divorce, and most of us will have to work in the business world to help support ourselves, and our families. Will we become successful businesswomen? Some of us will dominate our career paths while others will only stroll along waiting for something *big* to happen.

The dominant ones become powerful modern women whose names are well-known in their career circles. The others become the supporting cast that wane in the background. What does it take to become the "star" of the show? What characteristics do powerful modern women have in common?

In this chapter, we will first look at these common characteristics of the powerful modern woman. Then we will explore the setbacks that keep most of us from becoming successful in the business world. And finally, we will discover that a "shift in attitude" must happen if we as women will survive on the career path.

Common Characteristics

The powerful modern woman. What does that mean? I think to describe what the modern powerful woman is; we have to look at the word "powerful."

According to Webster's dictionary, the word "power" means—"strength, energy, authority, control, mastery, influence, leadership." What a complete word "power" is! If we want to describe what a powerful modern woman is, we have to look at the definition of the word "power" and see what characteristics these women have in common.

Strength—When I think of the word strength when it pertains to powerful modern women, I'm drawn to "strength of the mind." It is a fact of life that women are not as physically strong as men, but because of this, they have adapted their lives to have a large part of their strength in their mind instead of their body.

Powerful modern women have self-esteem which comes from their inner strength. They have strength of the soul. They have strength of the heart. They have a firm belief in the inner good of others.

I have met so many women in my life that are so strong with their thoughts and feelings, but don't have the skills or the tools they need to become successful in their careers or at home. However, when you suggest to them to become a mentor, to write these words down, to help someone else with their knowledge on that subject, they fail to do so. Why? Lack of self-esteem? Self-doubt? Fear of what others will say about them? They let their negative thoughts consume them and rule their lives.

This book will give you the skills and tools to take that inner strength that you have and to open it up like a caged animal. An animal that has been captured for too long. An animal that wants and needs to get out of the cage and explore this vast world that we live in.

Powerful modern women have this strength. They possess the inner drive and ambition that it takes to meet that impossible deadline. They use their drive and ambition to move up the corporate ladder and to take on bigger and more difficult projects. Their inner strength is one of the most important characteristics that powerful modern women have.

Energy—Powerful modern women have struck the balance of energy between what's needed to succeed in their personal lives, and what's needed to succeed in their business lives. These women use their wit, charm, and cleverness to find the quick, and sometimes overlooked solutions to the tasks facing them. They don't try to be everything to everyone. They've learned the word, "No." You can't be June Cleaver at home and then be Oprah Winfrey at work. That's just not realistic. But powerful modern women have learned that they can be great at many things, but not great at *all* things.

There is both energy of the body as well as energy of the mind. Let's face it; most women lack the energy of the body. We allow our world around us to soak up every ounce of energy and spice that we possess by doing our everyday tasks. We take care of our homes and families and don't have a lot of energy in reserve to concentrate on ourselves. Then when we want to make a contribution at work or with our friends and families, we don't make the effort because we're too tired to do so.

As Americans we consume more calories than other nations on a daily basis, yet we never seem to have enough "spunk" to last until the end of the day. We also spend most of our day doing things that won't make us healthy. We need to think of our mind *and* body as one. Both are very important in maintaining enough sustenance to do what we want in life. We need to eat healthier and we need to exercise.

I can't make you exercise your body because obviously I'm not there with you as you are reading this, but I do want to exercise your mind. If I help to take care of your mind with the tools and skills that I teach throughout this book, you *must* keep your end of the bargain—exercise your body.

Take the kids for a walk—clear your mind of all of the stress that's pressing on you today. Or go to the gym and read the rest of this book to stimulate your thoughts and levels of vigor. Do some stretching in the hallway as you're waiting in line to see the boss. Whatever it is, it will increase oxygen and circulation and will keep the body going strong for the rest of the day.

Another way to increase your strength is to eat breakfast! I know, our mothers were right about making us eat that first meal of the day. If you start your day with some carbohydrates, fiber, and some protein, you blood insulin levels will be stable until lunch or your midmorning snack. You won't feel like you're ready to break the person's arm in front of you in the restaurant line, and you'll find that you'll eat more often and in smaller quantities.

Powerful modern women understand that they need to accomplish a long list of things each and every day so they can stay on top of their game. To do this, they understand that they must eat right, and find the time to exercise a few times a week. Not only will this strengthen their bodies, but it will also build stamina of their minds. When your mind can focus on exercising your body, it tends to relax and the stress from our lives just melts away.

Exercise of the body and the mind must be done consistently if it is going to become a lifestyle change. If this is just the newest fad for you to join a gym or eat healthier until you lose a few pounds for a special occasion, you won't want to continue. Make these changes to make yourself a better person. Make these changes to make yourself a healthier person. Make these changes for yourself, not anyone else. If you do that, you will know that deep down inside your soul that you can accomplish anything. Powerful modern women understand the importance of strength.

Authority—In the "olden days," women were supposed to be submissive. They were supposed to be the support and nurturer of the family. They were supposed to be the "woman behind the man." They were taught only certain skills that would keep them from expressing their thoughts and feelings to the public.

I'm not sure why it was like that, or why it still is like that in certain parts of the world. I can only imagine or guess that it's all because of fear: fear of different ideas and points of view, fear of women who are biologically more complex than men taking over the dominant role in the household. Whatever reason(s) there are for this behavior, I don't buy into it one bit. I don't believe in it. It takes a man and a woman to procreate—equally. It takes two people to raise that child. Why wouldn't both parties have equal say in the opinions of the world, or how their lives should be spent?

Women of earlier decades learned that if they wanted to become successful in the male-dominated business world, they needed to gain some authority. They needed other people to not only listen to them and their opinions, but to trust the fact that they knew how to get the job done. This authority created power, and today's powerful modern woman creates that authority for herself and uses it whenever she can.

If you want to be a powerful modern day woman, you had better form some opinions on issues that you have some knowledge about. And you had better stand by those opinions when you're thrown into public situations. Don't hide in the corner when you know what the answer to the question is. Be proud and dignified. No matter how big or small. You can become the "queen" of the nest!

Grab a newspaper, and read the latest issues or debates. Read what is happening to children and issues that affect you and the people in your community. Take a night class, or go back to college to learn about a subject that you're passionate about. Only then will you have the strength and the energy to pursue your goals in life. When people can see "passion" on your face, and hear it from your voice, only then will they believe in your authority. Powerful modern women understand the issues of their communities both at work and at home. They know the facts, and they use this knowledge to make their contributions in all areas of their life.

Control—This is where the mentality of living in the man's world comes into play. This is where the title of the book comes from. *There's No Crying in the Man's World*—this has to always weigh on the powerful modern woman's mind. If you let your emotions get the best of you, there will be no respect for you in the business world. Men will look at you as a weakling, and they will not respect any of the original ideas that you possess.

Men don't cry when things go wrong for them, especially in the professional world. Powerful modern women realize that not everything needs an emotional shadow. Things can get done without getting so upset that crying is necessary to vent all of the day's frustrations and anxiety.

The powerful modern woman focuses on logical, rational thoughts, and knows that she will be ok once this difficult moment passes. You must focus and have strong concentration when obstacles are in front of you. You must take a deep breathe, and jump right in, feet first. But you must have a level head and demeanor about you if you want to succeed.

Once you have control over your "emotional tripwire," you then can master how to control other things in your life with the same steadiness and conviction. Once you have control over your mind and your spirit, then you will see doors of opportunity open right in front of you. Only with control can you see other opinions and viewpoints, which in most cases, will allow you to solve a lot of problems from a managerial angle.

The powerful modern woman uses this control to gain both respect and insight in her immediate surroundings. With these insights, her natural instincts are heightened and she can give projects a "woman's touch." But only if you control your thoughts and feelings can you move onto the next level of achievement. Control is the most critical of all criteria that leads you to becoming a powerful modern woman. Without control, you will never take the next step towards your goals, because you won't be able to focus on the obstacles and have clear thoughts on how to defeat them.

Mastery—You must gain both knowledge *and* experience to become a master of a certain subject or situation. It takes many years to become great at parenting, learning a craft, or even overcoming an obstacle. Too many people think that power is gained easily or quickly, but you must become an expert in something before respect or mastery is achieved. Mastery is needed before influence or leadership can be obtained.

The powerful modern woman understands that hard work is the only way to dominate her career field. But she knows that it takes time to learn the skills that her field requires. This takes a lot of energy and a lot of effort, but mastery of a skill takes both. There are no short cuts. There are no easy roads. All powerful modern women must become masters of their domain. They have to be the best if they are to compete in the male-dominated business world.

Influence—Once you control your thoughts in many different situations, you gain respect and "influence." Other people will look up to you and ask for your opinion, because they know that you're "walking the walk." They know that you've sacrificed many things to be in a position of expertise and authority.

However, with influence comes the need for mentorship. Powerful modern women share their thoughts and influence with other young women. They feel a responsibility to help other women fulfill their dreams and succeed in the business world. They also understand the importance of experience, and how it can help others accomplish their goals. This is what someone's influence can do. It can make a difference in meeting a goal or finishing a project. Influence means that you know your stuff, and others will confide and trust you to help them in critical times. All powerful modern women know that their influence can make or break their success.

This is one of the main reasons why I wrote this book. With the skills that I will teach you later in this book and future courses, I can help other women use the skills that I've learned along the way to help you achieve success in life as well as your career. I've had so many women ask me how I've achieved so much in such a short amount of time, and the only answer I can give them is that I've surrounded myself with people who've "walked the walk," and have lived to tell me about it.

Leadership—This is the combination of all the traits of power. Without the drive, you can't acquire the knowledge. Without the knowledge, you can't demonstrate your calmness under pressure. And without your calmness under pressure, you can't demonstrate the leadership that others want to follow. There's not one powerful modern woman today that doesn't posses great leadership skills. These skills don't just happen. They are learned at different stages of one's career. Whether you're a great parent, wife, or professional, leadership skills must be learned and mastered. The ability to influence others, to change the opinions and trends of your community is so important in today's world. But not everyone has that ability. Powerful modern women do. It's a culmination of all of their hard work that comes together to make them a driving force and leader in their career field.

Setbacks

When we look at women today, we must ask ourselves why some women live out their dreams while others watch them from the sidelines? What are some of the obstacles that all women face on a daily basis that prevent most of us from becoming the success that we all want for ourselves? There are many reasons why you stop yourself from doing the things that you really want in life, and I want to take a look at some of them.

Fear. Fear of the unknown is one of the greatest fears of them all. What if I fail? What if someone doesn't like me anymore? Whatever it is that is stopping you usually is related to some type of fear. But if you're not happy in your current situation in life, then you must change the things that you're doing now. This will require courage and stubbornness.

You must *focus* on your end result, and know that you will encounter hurdles, and *expect* to get around them. If you acquire not only the skills that you need to take the next step and a mentor to show you how to use those skills, then how can you fail? You have to have self-confidence. You must rely on your preparation and your guidance to get around the obstacles in front of you. If you do that, you'll definitely succeed!

Negative environment. Most of the people around you are comfortable with their own lives, and with where you fit into it. They are afraid of change. If *you* begin to change what *you're* doing, then *they* think that *they* have to change what *they're* doing. This fear leads to negativity, and they express this to you as criticism and doubt. They will try to talk you out of it, and you must stop them dead in their tracks.

If you want to make the changes necessary to take your life to the next level, then you need to block out all of the negativity that will surround you. You must step out of that environment, and surround yourself with people that are doing what you want to do. Oranges like to be with other oranges. Millionaires like to be around other millionaires.

This is the only way you can learn what the lifestyle is about. I'm not telling you to forget all of your old friends and family, but you must have some type of interaction on a daily basis with people who are at the level that you wish to obtain. If you don't spend time with this certain group of people on a continuous basis, your "usual" crowd will start filling your head with concerns and doubts, and will "rain on your parade." Don't let that happen!

Powerful modern women learn skills from other leaders in their environments. They position themselves in a way that they can learn these skills quickly, and then pass them onto others to achieve their goals. But to become a powerful modern woman, you must do the same thing. You must put yourself in a position to learn what the other leaders of your company know, so that you can become one of them.

Confidence and Self-Esteem. Yes, you are worthy! Yes, you have the ability and motivation. Yes, it will take a lot of work and sacrifice, but isn't it worth it if you can make more money, or have more time to spend with your family? What are you waiting for?

I don't know why women have a problem with self-esteem. No one will ever give you anything in life that she doesn't think you deserve. Why are you letting someone else dictate what she thinks you deserve?

Powerful modern women know that they must believe not only in their knowledge, but also in their instincts on decision-making. If they second-guess every decision that they make, then others will lose faith in them. It's only through confidence and knowledge can one succeed in the business world.

Laziness or Procrastination. A common problem that we all face in life is a small word I like to call "laziness." Laziness is the enemy to the powerful modern woman. Laziness can make any obstacle seem impossible to overcome.

Another word I don't use very often is "content." If you're content or happy in the place you are, you will *never* achieve the next level. Whether the next level includes marriage, kids, or a promotion, if you are truly happy at the stage your life is in right now, you won't have the attitude or the ambition to keep evolving. I'm not telling you to not enjoy the moment, or bask in the rays of your success, but I don't want you to live the rest of your life on past achievements either. I don't want you to be that older woman who always talks about the night she became prom queen. I always want you to focus on accomplishing the next step, and keep your head up looking forward to the next one.

If anyone knows about laziness or procrastination, it is I. I was notorious for this. I always studied and crammed until the last minute, and there never was enough time to get everything into my head. Don't be that way! You must take little steps everyday so that you don't get overwhelmed with the big picture. Powerful modern women take each day one at a time. They understand that each day may pose a problem that they must work around. The difference between them and those that fail is that powerful modern women expect the problems and obstacles while other people don't.

If you wait for tomorrow to get started, you may never get to it. Get off your butt today and do something that's necessary to meet your next goal. I don't care how small it is, if you just do something or change something, then your mind will know that you're serious about making changes, and that you've already started. Change something today to prepare yourself for the steps you need to take tomorrow. Start today!

Waiting for Someone Else to Do Something. Why are you waiting for someone else to dictate your future? "If I wait for Tom to get that promotion, then I can move into his spot." *No, no, no!* This is the wrong attitude! The powerful modern woman does not allow her own life to be controlled by the actions of others. The powerful modern woman makes things happen for herself and her loved ones!

You must prepare yourself and proceed to the next step on your own terms, and in your own time. Remember that you are *always* in control of your own actions. If you allow fear, negativity, self-doubt, or laziness to overwhelm you, you are defeating all of the dreams and goals that you've worked so hard for. If you want to take the next step in your life, you cannot be concerned with the actions that other people are taking. These other people are just doing what they have to do to take *their* lives and careers to the next level. Do the same thing, and concentrate on yourself and what you want. Powerful modern women believe in themselves and step up to the challenge when it's in front of them. Don't wait for someone else to make a move; take some responsibility and gain the knowledge that comes with the project at hand.

These five areas above can squelch any dream or goal that creeps into your head. You *must not* let that happen! The powerful modern woman must take a look at the rules of the boys' club (business world) if she is going to survive in the man's world. By defeating procrastination, self-doubt, and negativity; powerful modern women can take on the rules of the world that have been set by men.

If you think about it, we are our worst enemies, not men. Men don't look at themselves and have self-doubt about their abilities in life. Why do we have them? Women look at themselves and hate the way they look, hate the way they act, and hate the way they want to be. Powerful modern women do none of these things. They possess the confidence of men so that they can survive in the male-dominated business world. But how do they gain these attributes?

Shift in Attitude

The powerful modern woman looks at the world through different eyes as her other female counterparts. She can see the open doors that lead to ongoing possibilities and opportunities. But how does one develop the mindset of a powerful modern woman that is needed to succeed in the business world? And further more, how does one begin to think like a powerful modern woman?

1. Change Your Attitude—Your thoughts are a culmination of your subconscious. Powerful modern women think positive thoughts. These positive thoughts can lead to positive actions that give them enormous opportunities for success in the business world.

Even through obstacles that are in their way, these women envision the end, which includes getting through the obstacles. When you can think through your obstacles, and can clearly see the end of your project at hand, only then will you get through the obstacle. It takes careful strategy and planning, but powerful modern women learn through experiences from other projects that they will get through their problems.

Simply by changing your attitude towards yourself and your environment, you can then begin to think like a powerful modern woman. Your attitude is just a state of mind, an expression of your viewpoint on a certain subject. If your attitude is just a state of mind, then this means that it can be changed. Think positive, and you will develop the insights that you will need to get around all of the obstacles that will be in your way. Only then will you think like a successful woman.

There has to be a shift in the attitude of most women today. They are encouraged to live out their dreams, but somewhere between childhood and college, most women's self-confidence goes out the window. Why? Maybe it's because most young women lack the mentorship sources that are readily available to most men. Maybe they grow up wanting to get that infamous degree—the "**MRS**."

Whatever the reason is, the general attitude must shift towards self-motivation and self-confidence. All of the traits of a powerful modern woman centers on confidence and self-motivation. It is the belief in herself and her expertise that the powerful modern woman relies on in crisis situations.

2. Change Your Environment—The saying goes that you are a product of your environment. If you surround yourself with others that are depressed and are always talking about negative things, eventually this bad attitude will rub off on you, and other people will think the same about you. Is that what you want?

This is probably the level that you're at right now. Don't you want to change this? Isn't that why you're reading this book? Do you want to be like the rest of the crowd that's just going along in life aimlessly, or are you a powerful modern woman?

This book will open your eyes to new points of view. The rules of the business world (boys' club) are different than the rules that most women live by. If you can master the characteristics of a powerful modern woman and the rules of the business world, it will be no time before you'll be playing the game in the big leagues.

Think of this change in your environment as a lifestyle change. It can't be like a fad diet or a get-rich-quick scheme. Those things don't last and you usually end up in a worse environment then when you started. Change your surroundings, and learn the habits of the successful people in your field. Once you adapt these habits into your daily life, you'll realize that you're just like those people, and you will start to move your career forward very quickly.

3. Change Your Relationships—I don't know why we allow negative people to influence us so much. I can't tell you how many times I've heard other people tell me that I couldn't do something. Now that I've become so successful in life, I just want to shake those negative thoughts right out of those people. I want to ask them why they were being so negative and hurtful towards me. I want to ask them why they don't think I can succeed. Shouldn't my inner circle of friends and family be supportive and helpful in my endeavors? *Absolutely*! And I can tell you right now that my inner circle of friends and family that I share my thoughts and ideas with are the best protection I could ever find.

All powerful modern women have some sort of support group both at home and at work. They have people that they look up to that they use for their opinions. Powerful modern women rely not only on their own expertise on a subject, but also their support system. This support system helps these successful businesswomen strategize their next moves, and sometimes makes them see things in a different way. This helps to solve problems and obstacles quicker and easier.

Find people around you that you can trust. Find people around you that you admire, and ask for their help when you need it. You'll find that when you use your support group that you will expend less energy on projects than if you would do things alone. And you will learn new skills along the way from this group of people. They will have talents that you lack, and by using these talents, you will solve your problems faster.

4. Find Self-Confidence—Self-confidence seeps from every pore of a powerful modern woman's body. Every word that comes out of her mouth is met with certainty and action. She walks with her head held high and is always looking at what is ahead of her.

This is the attitude you must possess if you want to survive in the business world (boys' club). If you don't, they will eat you alive. They will tear you up and throw you to the side and worst yet, they will forget about you. If you want to be unforgettable, you must walk with pride, and exude confidence!

5. Use Your Experience—It's all about acquiring wisdom. That's where age and experience has us all. Wisdom is not the same thing as knowledge. Wisdom comes directly from intelligence *and* experience. This is why surrounding yourself with people who are at the level you want to obtain is so very important.

Just by surrounding yourself with other powerful modern women, you will learn skills that other people only can wish they could pick up. It's when you surround yourself with other successful powerful modern women that you can start to think like one. Once you start acquiring the thought patterns of these successful businesswomen, you will gain experience that will build the foundation of your own success.

You need to start somewhere, and powerful modern women understand that experience, as well as knowledge, are necessary parts of a leadership role. Both take time to acquire, and both build on themselves. Use whatever experience that you have to gain more insights into future projects. This will help you look ahead and avoid obstacles that may get in the way of meeting your goal.

6. Find a Mentor—Do you have one? Do you share your dreams and ideas with those that are the closest to you? Can you depend on them for support and straight answers without getting negative thoughts in return?

I mentioned briefly before about mentorship. I think that finding that one person to rely on and trust is so very important. As long as there is someone in this world who believes in your capabilities and dreams, that's all it takes: just one person, just one human being that connects with you, someone who thinks that you can achieve your goal. I don't care if it's a boss, a spouse, a parent, a child, a sibling, a teacher, or a friend.

There has to be someone in your corner that recognizes that twinkle in your eye when you talk about your dream or goal that you want to accomplish and encourages you to do it. You mentor is going to be someone who has already crossed that obstacle that you're about to overcome, and has lived to tell you about it. If you can find that one person, then you can consider yourself truly blessed.

I, myself have found several people that I know are in my corner. I look to them for both guidance and support in all of my adventures through life. Those people include my parents. My parents were always supportive during my academic years. My dad worked two jobs to help pay for my sister's and my educations. I always knew growing up that they were in my corner, no matter what happened. I just figured that was how it was for everybody. But I soon learned that not everyone grew up in a loving, caring household.

I guess for me, it was easy to become successful, because I had everything going for me, and how lucky I really am to have had that kind of environment to be raised in. Not everyone is as lucky as I was, and I know this. But what I want you to think about was what I had mentioned before—You *must* surround yourself with positive and inspiring people if you want to become a powerful modern woman.

There must be a shift in attitude first, a different way of looking at life. This "shift in viewpoint" is where your mentor comes in. He/she will show you how to focus on your immediate and long range goals, and will help you get to where you want to go because he/she's already done that, and knows the obstacles that will come across you path.

I know you're thinking to yourself—did she just tell me to get a male mentor? Unfortunately, it's still a man's world in business. Unfortunately, you still have to play the game as they play it, and who better to learn the rules of the business world than by asking a male mentor for help? If you can't find a powerful modern woman to become friends with, you need to find the next best thing—a successful male colleague.

But you can't find just any colleague; you must find one with all of the characteristics of being successful. If he/she is just part of the crowd and never comes up with original thoughts, then stay clear! Use these people to bounce ideas and strategies on just like successful business-women do each and every day. Trust in their opinions and listen to what they have to tell you. These people have been where you want to go, and hold the insights to the obstacles that are in your way.

When we look back through the characteristics of a powerful modern woman, we've learned that she is strong in body, soul, and mind. She sees the world as an opportunity to expand her horizons, much like her male counterparts. She has drive and ambition, and wants to work her way through the crowd. She thinks independently and without regret. She loves and respects those around her, and knows how to use their skills and unique talents towards the whole.

She knows and understands that she's been given an opportunity in this life to live her dreams, and she's willing to make sacrifices to get what she wants. She has a clear vision of the path that lies before her, and she knows what she has to do to follow that path. And if she doesn't know how to get to her destination, she knows who to talk to, and she surrounds herself with positive, successful people.

This book is dedicated to every woman that wants to make a difference in this world. It doesn't matter the age, race, height, or weight, we all can carve out our little corner in the big universe. We will learn what the rules of the business world (boys' club) are and how to shape our actions to beating them at their own game. We will be exploring

our emotional sides, and how they defeat our quest in becoming powerful modern women. We will learn how to set goals and how to reach
them. And finally, we will put everything we've learned together to get
ready to take the next step towards our dreams!

Chapter 2

The Next Step

We've identified the common characteristics of powerful modern women. We've learned what setbacks can get in our way from becoming successful, and we've also learned how we need to think in order to gain the wisdom that's needed to fulfill our dreams.

The next step has to do with getting in order your action plan. You've learned what the personality traits of the powerful modern women are, and now it's time to learn how to set your goals and achieve them. Each goal that you set will have different paths of obtainment, but you will see the same pattern that all goals are achieved. It's the same process no matter how big or small the goal is. In this chapter, we will help you to organize your thoughts to change, and we will show you how to create an action plan to put you on the path of achieving your goals.

Before I take you through the exercises that you will need to make your journey towards your goals a lot easier, I want you to go to the store and get a small notebook and label it—"GOAL-SETTING STRATEGIES." You can use one of those ringed binders. My only objective in this is for you to have something that you can write out your goals on, and keep them so you can plan out step by step how you are going to achieve them. Or you can jump on my website at www.Thereisnocrying.com to order your own goal workbook.

Section I: "The Perfect Day"

I want you to take out your notebook and a pen. I want to open your mind to the goal-oriented thought process by doing a little exercise I like to call "The Perfect Day." I want you to grab your pen, and write at the top of page the words "The Perfect Day." I want you to close your eyes, and imagine what your perfect day at work would be. Is it a day of hassle-free silence? Or is it a day that you land that big account that you've been working on for months?

Ok, now what I want you to do is to write down this perfect day on this first page. You can be as detailed as you want to be. In fact, the more detailed you are, the more specific your goals need to be to achieve that scenario.

After you've written down your "Perfect Day," I want you to re-read this. What did you write? What was your environment like? Was this a place that you normally see or have been to? Or is it completely different? If this "Perfect Day" was something that you live often, then this book is not for you. Obviously you have made choices in your life that your are comfortable with and are not regretful. However, if you go through your life in the normal, everyday world, and have never even come close to living the "Perfect Day" that was in your dream, then this book is *definitely* for you.

You are now beginning to see the way you can create a new world for yourself. By doing small exercises like this, you can start to see yourself in a different environment which can lead to changing major things in your life. This may include reaching a level of success, or earning more money. Whatever this "Perfect Day" is, you have to then find out the steps you need to take to make those thoughts a reality. This is the first step in reaching your "goal" in the business world.

Section II: Turning *Change* into a *Need*

Now I want you to take that "Perfect Day" and apply it to your life. Why is this the perfect day for you? You need to figure this out because without your reason for it, you will lack the motivation needed to keep on track towards it. Your reason for your "Perfect Day" is your inspiration for your dream. Everyone has "wants" in their life. I want this, I want that. These thoughts come and go. Yesterday you wanted a bike, but today you want a baseball. Most kids are into the "wanting game." They want everything under the sun, but what happens when they get it? They play with it for thirty minutes, and then it's thrown into the box with every other toy that they wanted for the past five years.

Do they need these things? Wanting and needing are two entirely different things. If you *want* something, you lack the inspiration or motivation to actually get it. Many things take some form of work to achieve, some type of sacrifice needs to be made if you are to achieve it. If you want something, you may or may not make the sacrifices that are needed to achieve it. But if you *need* it, you will do whatever it takes to get it.

This is why infomercials are so successful. This is why TV shows are so successful. They know that if they make you feel as if you *need* their products that they are selling you, then you will buy it. *Wanting* comes and goes, but *needing* gets the cake and eats it too!

You need to think about your "Perfect Day" and figure out why you need it, not why you want it. If it's a need, then you will do all of the exercises that follow in the book, and you will find the way to achieve this "Perfect Day." If you're flakey about it, you will start the process, and then lose your way because you will no longer be motivated to do it.

By thinking in terms of the big picture, you will slowly gain perspective on the steps needed to make that dream day a reality. Most people only dwell in their daily lives. They never are given the luxury of sitting down and thinking of the place they would love to be in the next few years. They only see their nose in front of their face. I want you to start to see beyond your nose. You *must* take off your blinders if you don't want to miss the opportunities that are all around you.

I have a little story to tell you. I always wanted to be a physician. I was a biology major and took all of the undergrad courses necessary to apply to medical school. I got to my senior year of school and took the MCAT entrance exam and realized that I was on the borderline of being accepted outright, or being put on the waiting list. I was devastated. I quickly realized that my dream I had for my life was about to change, and I didn't have a plan B.

I talked with my academic advisor, and he suggested going into something else like podiatry, optometry, or dentistry. I always enjoyed going to the dentist, so I talked with my old dentist that I grew up going to, and he convinced me to give it a shot. I took the entrance exam and waited for a call for an interview. I got a call for an interview at a school that was close to my house, but when I looked at my calendar, I had realized that I had an English final that same time and day of the interview.

My English professor was gracious enough to allow me to start later, and I set up the interview. I received my acceptance letter the next week, and I had to make a huge decision. Do I go through the interviewing process for medical school, or do I take a chance on the sure thing and go to dental school? I talked it over with my family and friends, flipped a coin, and decided to go to dental school. I can't believe what a great choice I had made! By looking at alternative pictures, I realized that I could still help people, *and* have my own office at the same time.

To this day I still believe that if you are prepared, life will throw you many opportunities. You may not know which opportunity is the right fit for you, but at least you will have choices. I want to talk you through this process in this chapter.

If you take anything from my previous story, it is that I thought that I wanted to spend my life doing one thing. In reality, I was better suited in a different regard. I always wanted to be a physician for the challenge and the prestige that came along with it, but what I didn't know was that this was just another emotional response to the thoughts that were in my head at the time. What I didn't know then was that I wanted to help people, but I also wanted to help them on my own terms. I didn't know that I would be a great business person and be a great solo practitioner. But I know this now. I love being on my own, and doing things I believe are the correct way. That independence would have been killed if I had gone to medical school and had worked for a group practice or for a hospital.

Sometimes you think that you want one thing, but you want it for the wrong reason, or it's not the correct thing you want in the first place. This is why knowing what you *want* and what you *need* are very important in this goal-setting process. I spent so much time and energy wanting something that in the long run, would have been very bad for me. It was a total blessing that things turned out the way they did.

Section III: Turning That *Need* into Reality

You must think of your "Perfect Day," and why you want your "Perfect Day" to become a reality. If this dream was just that—a dream, then I want you to rethink what you're really asking your heart to feel, and re-write your "Perfect Day."

If you can see the way you want to live your life in your head, then anything is possible. Our thoughts and dreams help to drive our ambitions. But some people are only dreamers. If you want to become a powerful modern woman, you must dream first, and then take the actions necessary to make those dreams a reality. Making something happen is one of the powerful modern woman's primary objectives. She understands that no one is going to give her anything in life, and she finds whatever solutions are out there to help her fulfill those dreams.

This is exactly what you need to do to make your needs into reality. If you feel strongly enough about your goal, that you must complete it, and then you will make the sacrifices necessary to meet that goal. These sacrifices could include spending more time at the office and less time with your family. It may mean that you can't go on that vacation that you've saved up for. But if you really need to fulfill this goal that you've put in front of you, you will find the way to do it.

Section IV: Finding the Problems

Have you ever met someone that complains about everything? The only thing that she has to say is negative and insulting. Usually this kind of person has many ideas that deal with how to change things or procedures around her, but she doesn't know how to communicate these ideas. She may have a problem with putting her thoughts into words, or she may be afraid of telling someone else who may reject her. Whatever the reason is, she uses negativity to shield her ideas. This is *not* a powerful modern woman's way of communication. If you want to change the environment around you, you must learn how to communicate your ideas to others.

You can do this by making a list of things you want to change around you. I want you to get your notebook and make a list of all of the things you want to change. Mark this page "Changes/Problems." Is your desk cluttered? Do you think there's a better way to communicate between your company departments? Do you think that your answering service is outdated? Whatever these things are, you need to write them down. Whether these things are personal or professional, it doesn't matter. They are all important. If you start to think about the things around you that you want to change, you will begin the process of creating solutions to these problems. If you are intelligent enough to recognize the changes that need to be made, then you are intelligent enough to solve the equations.

I have different employees all of the time. When a new employee comes into my office, I know it's just a matter of time before she approaches me about something she wants to change in the office. I like to try different procedures and ways of doing paperwork and dental techniques, but what I don't like to hear all of the time is a complaint about something we're doing. I don't want to hear the negativity, but what I do want to hear is a solution to the problem

they're having. I encourage my employees to go to continuing education classes and bring back different ways of doing things in the office.
Sometimes it's a product and sometimes it's a different approach to a
technique that we do. But you need to see the difference in the scenarios. Complaining only brings negative emotions. Creating solutions to
problems bring about change.

Section V: Creating the Solutions

Creating solutions to problems bring about their change. I want you to
go back through your list of changes that you want done. No matter
how long or short this list is, I want you to go to the next page in your
notebook, and I want you to start writing down all of the ways you can
think to solve these problems. I want you to mark this list as "Solutions." This may take you some time to do. There may be so many
things around you that you want to change.

Once you've got these solutions, I want you to look back at your
problems and solutions on the previous pages, and decide which ones
you want to tackle that pertain to you "Perfect Day." You need to write
down all of the different ways that will get you closer to your "Perfect
Day."

Section VI: Finalizing the Goal-Setting Process

Congratulations! You've just written down the steps you need to take
to reach your "Goals!" You imagined what your life "could" be like:
you noticed the changes that needed to be made, and you identified
the ways to make these changes. It's like the saying of "seeing the trees
before the forest." You saw the forest—your "Perfect Day" which is
your main goal. You saw the trees—the changes or problems that are in
your life that prevent you from reaching your main goal. Then you saw
the road in front of you that led to the trees and forest—this is your
path which is made up of the baby steps you need to take to reach your
goal—"The Perfect Day." Did you realize that it was this simple? Did

you realize that if you look at the big picture, and then take a step back and see all of the smaller things that are needed to see the big picture, that this process makes the big picture more achievable?

You just wrote down your main goal, your immediate goal, and the steps you need to take to obtain these goals. Guess what? Now they are achievable. Do you know why? They are achievable because you wrote them down. They are now physically in front of you. They are no longer a figment of your imagination. You've taken the first step. This first step is just like an alcoholic's first step in the twelve step program. She admits that she has a drinking problem. When she finally admits it and says it out loud, she consciously knows it is real. It is no longer in the corner of her mind. It is a real physical "thing," and now if she wants to control that "thing," she has to admit that it exists first.

Now you have these lists that are the first evidence that you have dreams and goals. Most dreams and goals are just passing thoughts in your head, but now you've got a physical list telling you that these dreams and goals actually exist. The list is real. This list can stare at you everyday.

Section VII: Taking Action

The next logical question is—"What are you going to do about it?" Are you going to let a lousy piece of paper with words on it defeat you? Are you going to allow those words that stick out at you, like an elephant in the room, get the best of you? I want you to say this out loud, and repeat after me—"*Absolutely not!*" If these words that are on this paper were not possible, then why did your mind think of them in the first place? Remember, as humans, we only use ten percent of our brains. Powerful modern women don't allow fear to get in their way of success. The powerful modern woman recognizes the goal that's in her mind, and will use those lists of solutions to take the action necessary to reach that goal.

When you go to the grocery store, do you just shop randomly or do you make a list? I *always* make a list if I want to be efficient and precise in my shopping. The times that I don't make a list, I end up forgetting at least three items that were the main reason for me traveling to the store in the first place. When you've planned your meals for the week, you need certain items from the store to make those meals for you and your family, right? How are you going to make those meals correctly if you can't remember all of the items you need to make them? If you can't remember all of those things, then how are you going to buy them at the store? You can't just buy some gingko biloba, and suddenly remember all of those things that you need.

So how are you going to achieve your goals, dreams, and desires in life if you don't write them down? How can you even remember if you've achieved any goals unless you have a list to cross them out? Without a list, our minds focus on other things around us: things that take up time, things that take us away from our main objectives in life, things that take us away from our goals, dreams, and desires. If you knew how to make these lists on your own, you wouldn't have bought this book, and you would already be a successful, powerful modern woman—You need to make that list. And I promise you that you will focus on those goals and restructure your life towards crossing those items from your list. Why? Because this list now exists. It lives on that piece of paper that you wrote it on.

Section VIII: Finding a Mentor

You now have your goals in mind, and you need to do a lot of preparation to get there. But where do you start? It's easy to have some words on paper that tell you what you want to do in life, but it's a whole other thing to put the words in motion.

Action is the only way to get started. But which problem do you solve first? Are these changes in a certain kind of order that will guide you down the path towards your "Perfect Day?" The answer is "yes," and it all starts with another person—your mentor.

I know I harped about finding a mentor in the last chapter, but this is the crucial step where a mentor can put your thoughts together and allow you to soar like an eagle. I know you're wondering where you can find a mentor. It's very easy. Close your eyes, and imagine you're in your "Perfect Day." Who is around you? What are they wearing? What is the atmosphere like? Are you in a corporate office giving a lecture on the trends that your company is experiencing, or are you finishing a huge project that took you half of the time that it did last year? Whatever your "Perfect Day" consists of, you need to find someone who is living that kind of lifestyle, and you need to talk with him or her.

I know that it's intimidating to meet new people or to meet people that are in a place that you want to be in, but I assure you that these people will feel flattered that you want to know about them. Take this person to lunch or have a drink with them. Trust me, everyone wants to talk about the most important person to them—themselves. Everyone loves to tell stories about herself and her past experiences.

You need to ask questions pertaining to your problems and solutions that you've already written down. Can you achieve these goals? If so, how did your mentor achieve them? Was there certain training or education that she had to take to get to the next level? Did she have to move locations? Did she have to change her eating habits or lifestyle habits? Where did she begin her journey and why? If you ask your mentor how to start your journey towards your goal(s), she will show you the shortcut to your "Perfect Day."

Why do you want to reinvent the wheel? Whether you meet this person once, or have a continuing relationship with her, your mentor will help you cut through all of the red tape, and tell you what you *don't* want to do. Your mentor will give you powerful insights that only one who has walked the walk will know.

When I got out of dental school, I started working for an older dentist on the other side of town from where I was living at the time. I was fresh out of school, and had no formal business education. I knew how to do dentistry but didn't know how to run my own practice. I remember I used to ask his advice on everything from diagnosing a problem to how to file an insurance claim.

I only worked for him for seven months, but those seven months prepared me for running my own business ever since. He taught me many ways of doing business and many ways *not* to do business. Since he was old-fashioned and I was wet behind the ears, I learned that everyone does things differently. I learned that I could use the core principals of business that he taught me, and incorporate my own twist to them. I wanted things to be more modern. I decided that I learned everything I could from him and I started looking for other people to learn from.

The one thing that I got out of all of this was that business is a non-ending universe. It is always changing, and if you don't change with it, you'll be left behind. Think of this first mentor as that—your first mentor. She will help you to put things into perspective. You need an outside unbiased person to see the skills that you have or lack, and to tell you honestly what you have to do to achieve the next step. Whatever your next step is, your first mentor will help you on your way.

When you begin to talk with your mentor, you should write notes down in your notebook. If you don't, you'll probably forget something significant. Don't be embarrassed—this is very important stuff! Your mentor will understand that you are serious, and will give you all the information you want. Just ask the questions and write everything down. Or you could get a digital recorder and with permission, can record your conversation. This way, you won't miss anything and can write down the main points in your notebook.

Now that you have your information in your notebook, I want you to look back at your own problems and solutions, and compare them to your mentor's. Were they alike? What was different? You need to sort all of the likes and dislikes out, and write an outline on the next page in the notebook called "Steps to (whatever your goal is.)"

This is the only way that you can get started on accomplishing your goals. You have to find a mentor that will show you what you have to do to go to that next level. Whether it's your friend who just got a promotion, or it's a trainer you've hired to help you learn different skills, you must have help. We're not all rocket scientists. We must learn the steps that are needed to meet our goals and then once we've reached them, we can give them our special and unique twists that will make them our own. But you do need some help, and finding a mentor will do the trick!

Section IX: Implementing the Characteristics

Make these ideas into an outline, and call this page in your notebook—"Steps to … (whatever your goal is.)" This list may be short or it may be long, but now you know exactly what you must do if you want to make a change in your life. Do you have what it takes to take these steps? To improve yourself and educate yourself? You've admitted that there are problems in your life, and now you have the path mapped out right in front of you on how to solve that problem. WOW! Is this powerful or what? I'm getting chills just thinking about how empowered you're feeling right now! As Emeril Lagasse would say, "This isn't rocket science!" This is called evolution!

Bacteria are just bacteria until their environment changes. Then they either have to change by mutating, or they die. This is called survival of the fittest. Our society as a whole had changed so much over the past generations, and it has done it because people's thoughts and ideas about their environments have changed. One thought leads to another, and when you look back on what you used to be even a year ago, you don't even recognize that person anymore. It's called evolution as a whole, but it's called "personal growth" for you. If you want to change; you need strength of mind, body, heart, and soul. All powerful modern women have that strength. And you do too!

As I look back on my adolescence, I realize that I grew up as a daddy's girl, maybe not as the phrase intends it to be, but I shadowed my father all of the time. I loved fixing things, and my dad was a mechanical engineer, so he liked to fix things too. He'd take me out with him to work on projects and always listened to the things that were going on in my life. He always encouraged me to do whatever I wanted to do in school and in business. I always felt strength from him and my mom, and as an adult, I feel that strength in myself.

Strength doesn't happen over night. You must work on your mind, body, soul, and heart a little bit everyday. Eventually you will feel strong enough to take action on your game plan. It's just like an Olympic athlete. She knows that her ultimate goal is the Olympics in her sport, but she must practice and gain strength in her mind and body everyday. She *must* practice everyday until there's enough repetition in her movements that her body and mind goes to that particular position more times than not. By doing these exercises, you are practicing mental clarity and concentration on changing your life for the better. And it takes time. And it takes sacrifice. And sometimes life stinks, but if you work at it a little bit everyday, you will feel confident that you will achieve your goal, and you will feel the strength of being a powerful modern woman!

I also understand that some of you may not have a lot of money to gain the education you need to get your degree, or you have a family that takes up a lot of your time. But if you want to make a change, you're only hiding behind excuses. And why are you hiding? What are you waiting for? I promise you that your children will respect you more if you're doing something for yourself too! Please, there's no time for excuses!

Now is the perfect time for you to make your move. You've identified your "Perfect Day" and how to get there. You've got your outline right in front of you. Now you need to start on step number one, and once you've accomplished that step, you must cross it out. Remember, you can't go back; you've already come too far. It's like that old saying about the rubber band—once it's been stretched, it never goes completely back to its beginning position—neither will you! You are now on your way to accomplishing your first goal! Go for it!

You will come across many obstacles while you're trying to make your "Perfect day" into reality. That's ok! Life happens. But you need to remember the characteristics of powerful modern women to help keep you on track towards your goal.

The first characteristic that you must implement into your journey is to have a great attitude. If you're starting to feel negative, or you're losing your ambition/drive, then take a step back and figure out where this negativity is stemming from. Is your spouse giving you a negative opinion about your new self-improvement project? If so, you need to explain to him that this is what will make you happy and that you want to improve yourself so that you can make better contributions to your marriage and family. If he is not in agreement, then you need to take a long look at your relationship and see if it's the best thing for you.

Another critical thing that you need to access is your energy level. Are you tired? Sometimes when we start something new, we go all out all at once and then we run out of energy to see it through. It's like the diet thing. Instead of making a lifestyle change, we go out and starve ourselves and eat nuts and twigs until we're finally skinny! The only problem here is that we're tired, skinny, *and* hungry! Then we rest, we don't exercise, we eat like crazy, and we gain all the weight back. This doesn't work. If you're tired, take a break for a few days. Get some sleep. Go do something fun. If you don't play, you won't want to work!

If you can take small steps, one at a time towards your goal, you will have the energy *and* keep the great attitude that you will need on your path towards your "Perfect Day!"

Section X: Review

As you go through the steps, you need to meet your goals. Sometimes you need to reread your lists and make changes to the list as they are needed. Sometimes your goals get sidestepped like mine were.

My main mission in life was to help people. I went through the pre-med program and discovered I didn't have the grades for medical school. After I took the blinders off, I realized that I could help people and still be in the medical field by doing dentistry. I combined my humanitarian desire with my independent nature and my love for gadgets.

My plan "B" ended up being the best thing for me in the long run. This is the main reason that reflection works. Sometimes you think you want one thing, but in the end, you get something different and better. You must stay focused on your goals, but be prepared to be flexible. You will still arrive at your "Perfect day," but some of the details in that image may be a little different than what you had thought they would be in the beginning of your journey.

You must be prepared for anything and everything. Your mentor gave you her story of how she arrived at the place that you would like to be, but there are so many outside factors that are uncontrollable. Two of these factors are timing and luck.

Let's say you want that promotion in your company that you've waited for a year to get. Maybe your company has decided to eliminate that position and redistribute the responsibilities to other people in that department. What will you do then? You need to have flexibility to look inside yourself and what you really want. If you want to indeed make that next step, then maybe it's the right time to look for another position in another company. Remember that when one door closes, another one opens. You must recognize that timing and a little luck help all of us throughout our lives.

Sometimes you'll come into contact with another person who can have a significant impact on your future, and when you first meet her, you don't have a crystal ball to see into the future. If all of the forces of nature are right, your timing will be right too, and you'll get what you want. If not, be patient and take your blinders off. Start networking with your friends, and see what's out there. If you're not paying attention, you may miss your door of opportunity. But you have to think outside of your path sometimes.

Section XI: Plan for the Next Goal

Just like the Olympian athlete who is learning new tricks of the trade to complete her routine for the Olympic games—you too will learn the different skills needed to reach your goal. But what do you do when you reach your first goal? That's right-you start the process over, and begin taking the steps necessary to meet your next goal. Welcome to progress, young lady!

Just like the athlete who practices her sport everyday, her positions and routine become automatic. After some time practicing her moves, their mind and body automatically go into the right spots to success-fully fulfill her objectives. The same thing will happen for you. Once you use the exercises we explained earlier in the book, and accomplish your first goal, you will have confidence and experience with the goal-setting process. The next step will be to make a whole new set of goals and figure out how to meet those goals. This will get easier and easier to do every time you take that next step.

I went through eight years of higher education. After I graduated with my doctorate, I swore off reading for a whole year! I was so burned out from the daily wear and tear of school that I felt relieved that I knew everything about dentistry and that now I would live on easy street and not learn anything else. Boy was I mistaken!

After awhile, I started to read those pesky journals that always came in the mail every month and realized that there was a whole new world out there for me to explore. I realized that dental school taught me 1975 dentistry and there was twenty-five more years of dentistry for me to learn. Then when I took the job with my neighbor next door, I real-ized that dental school taught me nothing about the business world! I feel like I've been playing catch-up ever since! I took off the "student" blinders that I had on for so many years, and discovered a huge uni-verse that had so many interesting things and people in it. I started to learn how to cook and picked up a little Spanish by watching the Mex-ican soap operas on TV. These new "interests" I had weren't necessar-ily career goals but were personal growth issues that I wanted to incorporate into my life. Now I'm interested in marketing and speaking engagements. Without those blinders, I've realized how lucky I really was to explore my dreams and desires, and now I feel compelled to help others do the same thing. That is one of the main inspirations for writing this book—once the student, now the teacher.

I thought that everyone was considered equal and that the women who didn't expand their horizons were just lazy, but now I know that they may not know where to begin, and they look at the big picture, and are overwhelmed with the thought of it instead of breaking it down into smaller parts.

Trust me, if I can do it, anyone can. I wish you the best of luck with your adventures! I know you can do it. Deep down you know you can do it too! Be prepared for the goal you want now and the goals that you will want in the future. The process will get easier and easier every time you complete it until it is automatic.

Section XII: Get Rid of the Excuses

I can't finish this ultra important chapter without talking about the negative side of changing your life. This negative side will try to convince you to go back to your usual way of doing things. This negative side will put thoughts into your head when you're at your breaking point. But since you know that you're like that darn rubber band, and you can't go back to your old life, you cannot let those thoughts ruin your momentum. Let's go over some of those thoughts that the negative side will put into your brain. All of these thoughts to me are considered nothing more than excuses! Leave the whining and excuses for the complainers of the world—you're a powerful modern woman and don't have the time for them!

Some women come up with the excuse that their spouse won't like what they're doing. Phooey! You cannot allow one of the closest people in your life to become negative towards your thoughts and dreams. Are they scared that you won't have time for them? Are they scared that you will leave them behind and move onto bigger and better things? Do they feel threatened by your success?

Whatever it is that you fear that they may say to you, forget it! Your significant other will love you for improving yourself and your environment. Most men do what they want to do—that's how they are brought up. They see something, and they learn to "divide and conquer." They don't think twice about asking what others "feel" about their situation. They run on instinct, and if you want to take the next step in your life, you must be the warrior and run on your instincts too. So what's in your gut? I've never went up against a woman's intuition. What does your gut tell you to do? Follow it and your significant other will too. If you believe, he will too!

Still others will tell me "I don't have the money." This is one of the biggest excuses there are out there. Most people see an object of desire such as a new cell phone, a new car, or a new pair of jeans as a "necessity." A lot of people will forgo paying their electric bill for the month, so they can possess this object of their desire. They make this object a priority in their lives.

These people don't realize that this object is a "want" not a "need." They can't see past the fact that this new object won't give them the freedom to get more objects or spend more time with their family. Education, more training, or making a change in your life are the only things that will give you more opportunities in life to live the way you've envisioned. "But I can't afford it." You can't afford not to! You've identified the ways that you want your life to change-now put your money where your mouth is. Just like food and water which are necessary for life, you need to make your education/training a necessity. This does include sacrifices. You may need to wait a little longer for that vacation so that you can do what you need to do to reach your next step in your life. But powerful modern women don't make excuses or say that they "can't" do something. Powerful modern women find a way to make it happen. Your child may not be able to take dance lessons for one year, but if you work hard this year and put all of your resources (money, time, and effort) into obtaining the skills that are needed for that promotion or new career choice, your child will be able to take more and better dance lessons after you make your career move. You may even be able to take time off to enjoy your child's recital.

Never live in the present. Always live for the future, because if you're always planning for the future today, you will never be disappointed at how it turns out. There are a lot of resources out there for those of you that can't afford training or college classes. There are student grants and loans for people who need it. That's why they are out there! The only thing that you have to do is ask around. Do you think that I had parents that just handed me over a free education? Not even close! They paid a quarter of my undergrad education, and I am still paying for the rest. But that was what I needed to do to get where I am today. I look at it as an investment in myself, and you should too. Invest a little today for you and your family's futures. It will all be worth it in the end.

Another popular thing to say is, "I don't have time!" I know, I know, you're too busy with your current life to make the changes necessary to succeed. Do you really want the success that you've already identified that you want? You took the time to do the exercises in goal-setting. You took the time in finding and spending time with your mentor. You organize your day and spend time doing the things you do for a reason.

Taking the time to educate yourself and setting your goals is very important, but it doesn't have to happen all at once. You need to do a little at a time. If it's a few hours a week, then that puts you closer and closer to your "Perfect Day." Don't burn yourself out. It's just like the fad diets that don't work or last. You must make a lifestyle change. It will take time to change the environment around you—it took time to make it the way that it is now, and it will take time to change it too. Be patient and work on it a little bit at a time. You will eventually reach your goal, but you need to take the time that's necessary to obtain the skills that are needed to take you to the next step.

Where do you come up with more time? It's a known fact that we as Americans spend an average of four hours in front of the television everyday! That's twenty-eight hours a week—over one full day that you're wasting on foolish stories about other people's lives. If you spent that time improving your own life story, just think of the progress you'll make in one week, one month, or even one year from now! Take some of that time for self-improvement and not waste it on entertainment. You'll find that you will have plenty of time to get everything done that you need everyday.

You must also be very organized with your time. Time management is a subject of many books unto itself. I want you to prioritize the way you spend your time. If you do this, you will find the time and energy that you need to improve your life.

If you have a spouse and children, you must organize your time so that you can spend some with them and have enough time to improve yourself too. You can't be rushed. You can't cheat your family so that you feel like you're being selfish. You must be organized with your time management so that you will feel good about the change that you're making. Once it's over, you won't remember what you spent your time on before you started on this quest. My bet will be that you'll realize you wasted a lot of your past few years and will make sure you don't waste anymore time doing trivial, mundane things. Look for the balance between fun and work and you'll find an abundance of time on your hands.

I've heard them all. The "I have a family to support, and I don't have the energy for this nonsense" thing. If you're content with your life, then that's great! If you live your "Perfect Day" everyday, then I congratulate you on your happiness and success. But if you're no where near living your "Perfect Day," then you need to look at your children and their lives, and figure out the kind of future you'd like them to have. If you want to stay where you are, because you don't want to do what is needed to take the next step, then good luck to you. You will never be truly happy unless you know that you're doing all that you can for you and your family.

I warn you that you're setting this kind of example for your children. They will grow up in an environment that's negative and mediocre. You'll live paycheck to paycheck, and set a lot of restrictions on their lives, because the time and the money won't be there for you to give to them. However, on the other hand, if you continue to improve your living conditions, you'll find that the more money that you're earning will buy your children more opportunities. Maybe your child is gifted in computers. Without extra money, he/she won't be able to nurture that talent and it will go to waste.

Don't you want that for your family? Don't you want to be able to afford a decent car so that your spouse won't have to spend his time and money taking the bus to and from work? Do you want to live in a safe neighborhood? Send your children to college? If you plant the seeds of hard work and resourcefulness now, your children will reap the harvest when they're adults. It's a win-win situation if you just do a little bit more everyday.

Your next worst enemy is yourself. If you say anything to the effect that "you're not good enough or smart enough" to take the next step—I will personally come to your house and shake these thoughts right out of your head! These are the most self-defeating words that your will hear—but you'll only hear them in your head. You must not let those doubtful thoughts control your destiny or your future. Those thoughts are just disguised as fear. Fear of the unknown. You must never let fear control your thoughts or actions. Whether this fear is from your own mind or someone else's, you must never let it into your heart. You've already come this far to allow negativity to squelch your dreams. Powerful modern women know that the path ahead of them is sometimes long and difficult, but they have the belief in themselves and their abilities that they will succeed.

You may not naturally have the talent to be the next Rembrandt, but you can acquire the skills necessary to be an outstanding artist. It's all in the training and practice. Remember that practice makes perfect, and perfection is not obtainable. Yes, it's a never-ending battle, but that's what life is all about. You struggle and claw your way into the world, and you do the same thing until you're out of it.

But don't allow self-doubt about your skills or your "worthiness" to dictate the outcome of your efforts. Yes, you will fail. But you will also succeed many times more. If you just keep trying, you will find the success and self-improvement that you've worked so hard for. That's all it's about. You'll see the obstacle before you, and you'll find whatever means there are to get over that obstacle. Then you'll take what you've learned from that past step, and you'll apply it to your next obstacle until you meet your goals. Then you'll make a new goal. It's a layered effect.

You build your house from the ground up. You are intelligent enough to learn the fundamentals needed to set goals and make changes. Don't allow negativity to keep you from your "Perfect Day!" Learn the common characteristics of powerful modern women and adopt them into your own personality. Soon enough, you will find that you possess the skills that they have, and you will meet the goals that you've set before you.

Chapter 3

Rules of Business

After you've learned the goal-setting process, you will learn that you're about to enter into a different kind of world than you're used to—the business world. This world has unique rules that will make or break your success. If you learn the rules and apply them to your actions, you will find that your career path will take a giant leap forward.

Knowing the Importance of the Rules

The importance of the rules puts everything into perspective for powerful modern women. If you're moving yourself into unknown territory, you'd better know what you're getting yourself into if you want to survive. Powerful modern women thrive on knowing the rules and will play them accordingly. Now is the time you put your skills to the test. If you can think the way men do in business, there's nothing that will stop you in this world. But make sure you know the difference between thinking like a man and acting like a man.

Some powerful modern women make the mistake of dressing in the three piece suit, talking trash, and smoking cigars with the boys—then she ends up making everyone around her uncomfortable and alienating herself from the crowd. I don't want you to act like a man, but I don't want you to be a pushover either. There's got to be a happy medium in knowing the rules of the business world, and how to implement them without offending anyone.

An example of the earlier alienation comes from my own childhood. I grew up with my sister in a small country town where there were no sidewalks. We lived near a corner of two main roads and all around us were boys. We were the only girls on that corner. My sister and I loved to play sports and found ourselves in the middle of many dodgeball, football, and basketball games. My mom stayed home with us, and would always make sandwiches and Kool-Aid for us during the day, and the boys in the neighborhood would come over everyday and enjoy the food and the activities.

This was all fun and games until high school when all the boys were after all the girls. The boys would still come over, but they weren't interested in playing many sports—they were interested in getting homework or asking me about one of my girlfriends. These guys would look at me and almost see right through me. I could feel it. Most of them were only interested in me to get information on one of my friends ("Is she seeing anyone?")

When I think back to those days, I realize that I became "one of the boys," and that's exactly how they saw me. They didn't or couldn't see past the "jock" and see the female inside of me. I enjoyed spending time with them but ended up alienating myself by doing so. They wanted to play ball with me, but wanted to take my friends out on dates. I don't want this to happen to you.

You need to learn the rules of the business world and follow the rules when you're playing in this world, but I don't want you to think you must act like a man to do it. Men are men, women are women. But when you're talking about business, business is above gender, and since boys have set the rules, we as women must follow those rules. There's just no way of getting around it. But there are ways of following the rules as women, and we're going to discuss this later in the book.

First we must define the rules. Let's take a look at the rules …

The Rules

Rule #1—Survival of the Fittest

Rule #2—Make Things Happen

Rule #3—Second-Place is the First Loser

Rule #4—There's No Crying

If you can learn these four simple rules and incorporate them in your thinking process as you set your goals in your career, then you are well on your way to becoming a successful powerful modern woman. Remember that powerful modern women become "masters" of their domain. It takes both knowledge of the rules *and* experience of playing the game to become a master in the business world (AKA the boy's club.) If you can start out in your business endeavors by knowing and playing by these rules, you will make more progress and more deals when you have to interact with men.

Men are very comfortable with other men when it comes to business. Why? Because they all know the rules of the game. When they were growing up, at some point they were taught what the rules were, and they were slapped on the back and told that they were ready to conquer the world. At no point in life was I slapped on the back and told anything. My father gave me as much advice as he could about the world, but he never sat me down and told me specifically what the rules were. I ended up learning them on my own.

Now I want you to learn each of the rules' descriptions and how to apply them in your business surroundings. If you can do this, you will find your path towards your goals less bumpy than if you tried to do things your way. Unfortunately it's the nature of the beast.

Rule #1—Survival of the Fittest

Yes, men think in evolutionary terms. They feel that only the strong will survive, and in a way, this is true. Let's look at politics, for example. There are many politicians out there that aren't the sharpest tacks in the box, but they still win the elections. Why? Rule #1 doesn't necessarily apply to the true meaning of the phrase in every situation. The *best* or most qualified candidate doesn't always win. But the person who is perceived as the best always wins. Which candidate is more personable? Which candidate represents the "popular" set of values and goals of the community? Whoever does this usually wins.

Perception vs. Ability

I know this doesn't make sense in most women's eyes, but it's true. Some CEO's start out in the mailroom and twenty years later earn the right to become CEO. Not because of perception, but because of their own abilities and efforts in their field. Other CEO's pull a few strings and end up at the top of the company because of *who* they know. This is one of the trickiest rules of them all. You never know which angle to use to meet your goal, so my theory is to know all of them. You must look at all angles of this rule if you're going to be ready to play the game in the business world. Let's review each angle together to illustrate the examples above.

The literal interpretation of the phrase "survival of the fittest" gives the impression of being the best candidate for the new position or promotion. You chose and set the goal that you want to accomplish and have identified the path you need to take to meet that goal. Part of being a powerful modern woman includes not only having the knowledge that's needed to meet this goal, but also to be an authority or expert in that field.

In my opinion, as a female trying to survive in the man's world, you must take things to the next level. If you're learning a new set of skills such as taking classes on becoming an effective public speaker, then you should not only take the classes on this subject, but practice these skills until you become an expert at them. It's the same mind set as the Olympic athlete. She practices her sport so much that it becomes automatic or second-nature to her. If you are the best at your new skill set, you put yourself ahead of the rest of the field when promotional reviews are done. When other men place judgment on you, you want them to look past your skirt and look at you as the obvious person for the promotion. You want them to be unable to deny you of this next step, because you are the most qualified.

I think the trouble business has had in the past had to do with the quotas that the equal opportunity authorities placed on them. They were ordered to have so many females in certain positions, but they were only put there because they were in the minority and not because they were the most qualified candidate for the position. This was not the best way of doing things. But that was then. We, as powerful modern women, don't want this to continue.

We want others to feel comfortable with us in their environment not because we were part of a "quota," but because we belong there based on merit. We want to dominate our career fields! I know that this means a lot of hard work for you to train and educate yourself in the ideas and skills that you lack, but if you want things bad enough, you'll do what it takes to get it.

Become the Expert

This leads us to the next angle which has to do with perception. Not only do you need to be the master of those skills, you must also be *perceived* as the expert. How do you do this? This is simple, you start "walking the walk."

In dental school, I was in my senior year, and I was starting to feel the pressure of finishing up my requirements to graduate from school and get a job at the same time. I wasn't sure where to go to find a job, and one of my instructors told me to try one of the clinics first. He said that I would get very fast at many skills and would learn new skills that would benefit me later in my own business. I told him that I wasn't fast at things but that I was very thorough. He told me that no matter what you do in life, sometimes you have to "fake it till you make it." That was my first lesson in perception.

As most young entrepreneurs and business owners, we start our businesses with the smallest amount of knowledge. Yet somehow we grow over the years and become very successful as business owners. How does this happen? If you seem comfortable in your own skin and confident in your knowledge and skills, people will also begin to feel the same way. Then when you get some practice at those skills, your expertise in that area will flourish. That's one of the main reasons the medical field calls their businesses "practices."

Everyday I practice the skill sets that I use. After I learn a new technique or procedure, I need to practice it, then after a few times of doing it, it becomes very comfortable, and I feel very confident in my ability to perform it. When this happens, I usually will recommend that procedure more, because I know that I can solve a particular problem by using my past experiences with that technique.

The same mindset can work for you but you still need to have the skills at some point during the journey. You can't "fake it" forever, so I would suggest that you be the best candidate for the job, and walk with your head held high, and be perceived as the best. This requires a lot of practice and sacrifice, but powerful modern women aren't afraid of a challenge, and I know you aren't either!

Connections

This leads us to the final angle of the rule—to know the right people. I can't tell you how many people in life get where they are by knowing the right people. It irks me! Too many people get away with things just because they have people in their inner circle that have influence over the outcome of the situation. I know this isn't fair, but unfortunately this is part of the business world.

Sometimes decisions are made based on "popularity" and not based on merit. This also isn't fair, but you must put yourself in the best position to win the next promotion or spot in your career. This means that you must be very diplomatic in your environment. This requires control over your emotions and behavior.

Most women love to gossip about other people or situations in their environment. You must control this habit. Men don't gossip about each other. They could care less what happens to the next dog as long as it doesn't affect the most important dog of all—themselves. You must approach each challenge as that—a challenge. You can't take things personally—business is business.

Powerful modern women know that if they can control their emotions, they will be able to see other opinions and viewpoints which can help them solve the tasks in front of them. If you can be perceived as friendly and diplomatic, more people will want to work with you, and this can lead to the "popular" vote. Once you possess the "popular" vote, you need to position yourself as the obvious pick of the people that make these decisions. Your mentor may be able to provide some influence in this area. If you want to take your life to the next level, you must find out who is part of that group and make your presence known. Maybe you volunteer to organize the company's next fundraiser. Or maybe you join a group practice or firm and position yourself as the marketing guru for the business.

If the "forces that be" know who you are, you are more likely to advance in your career. If you sit back quietly and hope that your efforts and merits will be enough to move you up a notch, you're dead wrong! As the saying goes—"He who shouts the loudest wins!" Start shouting! Think of a way to put yourself ahead of the pack.

You are dominant in your skills, you've mastered the art of politics, now you must also "campaign" for the position. Think out of the box. You may need to ask your mentor for some thoughts on the subject. She may be able to give you examples of what she did to move up the ladder.

If not, you have to think of something that will make you the dominant force in your position without being thought of as arrogant or difficult to work with. Even though you must be the best amongst your peers, you still have to be friendly enough not to scare them away. It's always good to have more friends than enemies! At some point in the future, you'll have to work with these people again, and if you burn your bridges, you will have more problems down the road. Be the best, but don't be arrogant. More people will stab you in the back and will call you derogatory names if you have a chip on your shoulder. You cannot be loved by everyone, but go for the majority vote, and you will win every time!

Rule #2—Make Things Happen

There's a big difference between what men and women think on this matter. Women think that things will happen, and everything will be alright. Men don't think that way at all. They don't believe that things will just happen. They make things happen. There's a big difference in philosophy on this one.

Take Action

Men are taught to be the aggressors. They are taught to be primitive and go out into the world and "hunt their game." They are taught to be assertive and make the first move towards their goal. If they want to move to the next level, they know that they must *act* on their wishes if they are to move ahead.

Women aren't naturally programmed that way. They are taught to wait back and see how things play out and usually there'll be room enough for them too. Again—*Phooey!* Powerful modern women cannot sit back and allow the world to pass them by. They must realize that if they sit back and only play defense, the other team (men) will run and score all the points in the world.

If a powerful modern woman sits back and doesn't show her presence in her environment, how will anyone know how special she really is? Powerful modern women know that they have to take action. They must set their eyes on their target and proceed forward. If they don't do it, who will? Men, that's who! That's what they are taught as young boys. They are programmed to be the main bread winners and to do this they know that they must make their presence known in their workplace. If they want to move up the corporate ladder, they will make whatever sacrifices they need to do, because they are confident in their abilities, and they know that it will all pay off in the end.

Women aren't necessarily bred that way. But as evolution progresses, our aggressiveness will too. It just takes a moment to decide to make a move. You've already gone through the goal-setting exercises. Then you learned the steps that you need to take to move towards your goal. Now it's your chance to take action! Now you must take that first step to make it happen. Don't follow your instincts on this one. Go ahead and take your first step! You'll soon learn that this is the most difficult decision to make, and once you do it, you'll be well on your way to achieving the next step in your career.

Create That Killer Instinct

We allow the excuses of the world to control our actions as well as our outcomes. "I'm not good enough, I don't have the money or time, or my spouse won't like it" all come to mind. It's interesting that if a man gets a promotion that will take him away from his family at times, he makes that decision with little thought or a second guess. A woman with the same opportunity will go through all of her environmental situations and excuses before she decides what to do. And most of the time, she will allow one of those excuses to hold her back.

Men aren't like that. They have that "killer instinct." To be a powerful modern woman, you need that "killer instinct" too. Every decision is not the last decision you'll make. Your next step may need to be drastic to make future steps that aren't so drastic. And remember that it's a woman's right to change her mind. If you make a decision that's not right for you or your family, there's always other opportunities out there. Powerful modern women always leave themselves an "out" if they need it. Never close the door completely on an opportunity or a person, because you never know when you'll need it/her in the future.

When I graduated from dental school, I decided to work for another dentist for a year. Then an opportunity opened up for starting my own practice. I knew the basic skills to do dentistry, but I didn't know a lot about the business of owning my own practice. I decided that I wanted to be on my own. I had confidence in my intelligence and the love for learning new things in my corner working for me.

I started my business on pure instincts and after three years in business, I decided to bring a professional in to help me. I hired a management company (McKenzie Management) to come into my office, get into my books, and tell me what to do. The management company was one of the best moves I ever made. The price tag was $20,000, but it turned out to be one of the best investments that I made to this date.

The management company showed me "basic business skills 101." They looked at every aspect of my business from profit and loss to how many new patients per month were coming into the practice. These were all aspects of the business that I didn't even know I could track. My first instinct (probably because I was a woman) was to go with the flow and see what happened. I did that for the first three years.

Then something got into my head that made me think that I could be doing much, much better and that I needed some help, like a mentor, in determining how to do this. I then went to a conference where the CEO of this particular company was giving a lecture and I liked what she had to say about practice management. I realized I didn't know anything about my own practice or how to control the numbers and decided to hire them for an evaluation and work-up.

After the management company taught me how to evaluate my numbers, they showed me how to set goals for the next year. Those methods were so valuable, because I could change things around and measure how my marketing and follow-up methods were working for my business.

I took the action necessary to follow the methods taught to me so that I could meet my goals that I had set for the year. And it's worked ever since. By learning these management skills, I learned invaluable techniques that allow me to analyze past performance and predict future performance. If I would have kept my go-with-the-flow attitude, I know that my practice would not be where it is today.

I learned an invaluable lesson on aggression. If I don't analyze my practice, who will? No one cares about my life and my career as much as I do. I'm glad I was lucky enough to learn this lesson at a fairly young age in my career. You will have to learn this lesson too.

If you won't take your career path into your own hands, who will? Remember that no one cares about your success more than you do. And no one else has as much control over your career success as you do. So don't wait around with the rest of the girls. Don't depend on anyone else to give you the things you want and desire. Go out and get them for yourself. You'll feel so empowered when you do that! You'll feel so appreciative of your accomplishments, and you'll feel so proud of yourself, because you earned your success. You didn't just have it handed to you.

Deliver

This brings up another word that comes to mind—the word "reliability." Successful powerful modern women are reliable. Others know that they can count on her when the chips are down. If you tell others that you are going to perform a certain task—please do it. Your credibility will be shot if you don't.

Other people, especially men will only deal with others that will get the job done. Most successful people don't have the time to harp on others for a task to get completed. People that aren't self-driven and aren't independent never become successful in the business world. To be successful you must be action-oriented. You must acquire your new skills, become a master at those skills, *and* perform those skills when duty calls you to do so. Only then will you become successful as well as a powerful modern woman.

You must deliver on your promises. You may not be the best at the task, but you must give one hundred and ten percent, or you'll never earn respect. And that's a key aspect of the business world. You must earn respect. Until it's your turn to step up to the plate and demonstrate your expertise, you need to stay in the background and practice your skills. Men like to see the skills that you possess. They don't necessarily want to hear about it. Remember, men still look at you as a woman, and for some reason, they are programmed not to "hear" the frequency of your voice. So if you're bragging about yourself or talking a lot of "smack" about the current situation that the company's in, then they will totally shut you out. Don't be a gossip. Step up to the plate and knock out a home run. Only this way will you earn their respect and open up the lines of communication that are needed to take the next steps in your career. Remember it's all a game, and you're learning how to play the rules of that game.

Rule #3—Second-Place is the First Loser

This next rule has everything to do with sports and competition which men have flowed into the business world. The reason why a lot of women don't understand the business world as a whole is because they've never played organized sports. For those of you that have ever played on a high school or college team, you'll understand the analogies that are set up in this part of the chapter. For the rest of you that have never picked up a ball in your life, I will go over the sports mentality with you so that you too will understand the man's mind.

Sports

Why are sports so darn important to the male species? Well for one thing, many sports incorporate the team aspect of business. Every business includes a group of individuals that must work together for the good of the company.

Let's break it down into the business that I know the best which is dentistry. I have the ability and knowledge to do every job in my office however; I know that doing this is counter-productive. It is more cost-effective and profitable if I divide the responsibilities of the office into sections. I have two women that assist me and the hygienists do our jobs by organizing and setting up the chairs for the patients.

The hygienists are in charge of cleaning teeth and taking x-rays. They go over the health history and are my first defense in detecting medical and dental problems. Then I have an office manager and an assistant who keep the staff orderly. They're in charge of billing and scheduling.

And then there's me who does all of the dentistry that comes into the office and helps to manage the staff. All of the ladies work as a team towards the goals of the office which are to maintain our patients' health and build beautiful smiles. Everyone is equally important in their contribution to the office. When one person is missing, it is up to the others to cover for that person to help make things run smoothly.

My team is exactly like a sports team. Every player has a job that she is to do. Individually, the players wouldn't be very effective in winning a game, because there's just too much to do for just one person. But if the players work together as a team, each player can perform her specialty, and they can get the job done. It's important to work as a team on projects; you will compliment each other and everything will be done effectively and efficiently.

Competition

Ego has a lot to do with sports too. Whoever is the biggest and fastest team usually wins. Winning is an easy way to confirm their superior abilities at certain tasks. It's the same way in business too! If your company is talented, it will be easy for it to expand its operations, which is great for you and the company's shareholders. But in business, if you lose, you usually don't get a second chance. If you lose on a team, there's always next year or next season to try to win the championship. If you lose in business, you may end up losing your livelihood, or worst yet, your company may go under. In business, there's no second place. You must be the best at what you do. If you're observed as an "expert," you'll always move to the head of the pack.

Teamwork

Another characteristic that team sports teach its participants is "sharing." Not only do you need to share responsibilities but you need to share your thoughts and ideas with your teammates. Experience is a very important thing in business as well as in sports. As with sports, a business hires you for the potential they see in you. They think that you possess a certain type and number of skills that are needed to deliver the company's objectives. But this is only a starting point.

There are many different levels of labor and management in a company's infrastructure. If you participate in their team efforts, you'll realize that if you share your ideas and thoughts on the task at hand, that along with other's ideas, the problems of the company can be solved, and their objectives can be met easier.

As the saying goes—"There's no 'I' in team." You must be a team player. It's your obligation to live up to the potential that the company hired you for. This requires you to master your skill sets, and, of course, you must learn new ones and practice them until they're automatic too!

Businesses see the world as many projects that they'll conquer one at a time. They do this because they know that every project has a certain learning curve associated with it. After a certain number of projects are completed, that team can then use the experience they've obtained from past projects towards future ones.

Experience is like any education—no one can take it away from you. Your company and its personnel use this experience and new ideas to help the company expand and become top dog. It all goes towards the common good, but you need to put yourself on the line and express your ideas. Powerful modern women believe in their abilities because of the experience and training that they've received. They know that it takes a village to raise a child, and they know that their contributions are important towards the team's goals.

Someday you will be called upon to be someone's mentor. This role requires you to do a lot of sharing. You'll share your opinions about the different experiences you've had in the past pertaining to different objectives made by your employer. By sharing your ideas and insight on different subjects, you're helping someone to broaden her horizons, and in turn, you're obtaining a perspective on the role that you play at your present position. This may help you see potential changes you'd like to make for your own career. If you share with someone, you'll always get something back in return. Be open, and let others use your abilities for the common good.

Each One with a Purpose

Another similarity between sports and business in the man's world is the word "organization." This is similar to the teamwork aspect where all of the members of the team need to work harmoniously together for the good of the team. When you hear of the word—team organization—it's just that. It's a large group of people that are working towards the common good of the team.

Your company is an organization. All of its members/personnel have specific jobs that all fit together to form the company's overall function. Everyone has a purpose. Someone knows how to "teach" others how to do their jobs—these are the managers. They have experience working in those positions that others possess for the first time. In the sports organizations, these people are the coaches of the team. It is their job to teach the players of the team how to play the game and to make sure they have the right mix of people that are needed to carry out their main objective (which is to win).

There are also other people that are important to the company such as supporting personnel (accountants and human resources). These people help to make sure that the company runs smoothly with the daily operations. Bookkeeping and employee problems all need to be satisfied if a company is to keep running.

There are also maintenance people and technical service employees that make sure the mechanical services of the organization continue to run. Especially in these days, there are many companies that use mechanical and computerized means to create their end products. These employees are critical to the survival of the organization.

And last but not least, there are all of the service people that include everyone from the cafeteria worker to the janitorial service employees. Without them, clutter and chaos would be rampant. These employees help tie together everything that the other employees do. They help to make the other employees' lives easier!

An organization can be thought of as a living organism. It is constantly changing and updating itself and its function and contribution to the world. All of the people that work for this company must change to keep up with the times and what the worlds' demands are.

It is very crucial to realize that you are very important to your organization. You do matter! Whatever your special skills are, you must share them with not only your company but also with the world. This is what gives you liberation. You are lucky to be in a society that will allow you to form and express opinions. You are lucky to be allowed to grow as a human being in and out of the business world, and to be able to interact with the world around you. Feel lucky and do something about it. Realize that you are a part of something bigger, and allow the other people around you to make you a better person. As you become a powerful modern woman you will feel this and so much more. As you become a powerful modern woman, you will realize that you must do your best for not only you, but for future generations after you.

Have a Plan

Sports are wonderful "planners." What I mean by this is that all sports teams have a "plan," and they do everything in their power to execute that "plan." Businesses are the same way.

In sports, your coaches analyze their teams' strengths and weaknesses and compare that to their rival teams' strengths and weaknesses. They then get a game plan together to see how they can meet their main objective which is to win the game. They watch film of other games. They show their players different plays so that maybe they can move the ball in a different way so that they can score more points against this other team. Businesses run the same way. They know what their competitors are doing, and they make their "plans" as to how they are going to beat those competitors.

They analyze the market to see what the consumers want and how much they are willing to spend on those products, and they get together a plan to make those products for their market. But they not only need to make the product, they must convince consumers that their product or service is better than their competitors' product by using different marketing strategies.

It's all about winning. If you can carry out your plan better than your rival can, you win. It's the same in sports as it is in business. And the beauty lies in the plan. Sometimes the plan is mainstream, and it works; and sometimes the plan is off the wall, and that works. Every time you're in competition or in the marketplace, it will be different. This is where experience will help. In certain situations, different methods work. Only with experience, will you know which method to use. And sometimes you must know when to cut your losses and come up with a different plan. Just like sports, business is all a game and you can't win unless you play.

Practice

Once you have a game plan put together, you must practice the moves that are needed to execute or carry out that plan. In sports, you practice different skills such as throwing or passing the ball, shooting the ball in the hoop, or hitting the ball. All of these skills are important if you are to win the next game. Conditioning is very important if you are to outlast your rival opponent.

In business, skills are practiced also. As I've said many times before, you must become proficient in the skill sets that you need to carry out your job. This takes practice and training. That's why sports teams have many different coaches. There are so many skills that need to be perfected for those teams to be successful in that sport. Businesses are the same. There are so many positions in a company that require different skill sets. You must master the skill sets needed for your current position before you can move onto another.

Remember that practice makes perfect, but perfection is never obtainable. Just like professional athletes, they must practice the fundamentals everyday. They will never become "perfect" at those skills, but they will be better than ninety-nine percent of the rest. You must do the same. You'll never be perfect, but you can be the best. Strive for being the best, and I know that your dedication will take you to your "Perfect Day!"

Just like sports teams, you must work with your teammates if you want to execute your game plan. You must share your ideas with your colleagues and contribute what you can to the overall objective of your company. It's a common saying that "he who fails to plan, plans to fail." Remember that there's no second place in business. If you want to succeed and move up to the next level, you must practice your skills and follow the plan of the company. If you can use your skills and incorporate them with your colleagues' skills, there's no way that you can fail. You will be very successful in business as well as in your life. Welcome to becoming a powerful modern woman!

Throughout this rule, I've tried to compare the analogies of sports and those of the business world. They are very similar, and if you can understand the general rules of a certain sport, you will be able to understand the general rules that men have made up in the business world.

If you want to see this comparison in action, my suggestion would be to watch a game sometime. Watch and see how the players interact with each other. See how the coaches interact with the players. Listen to the commentators interact with each other. The commentators analyze the strengths and weaknesses of each team and compare who is executing their game plan. It doesn't matter if you understand the rules of the sport. Just by watching the game, you will begin to understand the uniqueness of each situation and how each player or team as a whole adapts to that situation.

Rule #4—There's No Crying

If you talk to many men in business and ask them why they don't like to deal with women in business, they will tell you because women are emotional. I know, I know, it's not a fair thing to say, but it is true. When I was starting to write this book, I talked to my boyfriend and asked him that very same question. I asked him what other men think about women in general and he said the following:

> *"Don't listen to women because their estrogen gets in the way."*

> *"Men feel like women are too emotional to make logical decisions."*

> *"Women always define everything and sometimes things aren't definable."*

> *"They're always crying—whether they're happy or sad—it just doesn't make sense."*

> *"We were born and bred to believe that women can't make better decisions than us."*

Now I love this man dearly, but I couldn't believe that he said the things that he did. I thought that we were in the 21st century and that women were equal to men, but that's not what it sounded like to me. So I analyzed what he told me and came up with a few things that I want you to know so that you aren't thought of in this way. (And remember that not *all* men think this way.)

Gossip Queens

As I've said before, many women are just plain gossip queens. It is in our primitive nature to know all of the rumors about the people around us and to spread the rumors to those that don't know them yet.

I, myself have a tendency to listen to the rumors and give my "two cents' worth" about them. Why are we like this?

I think it comes from ancient times. The men would go off and do the hunting and building of the communities and this would leave the women and children to hold down the homesteads. Most of the women shared responsibilities such as cooking and raising the children. Naturally these women would talk in groups and pass on the community and family stories to each other and the children. As societies changed and matured, the style of communication amongst women changed too. Men would take their families across deserts and mountains to find land and a better way of life. Women weren't living in the close-set communities that their ancestors once lived in. Most women in the 1800's were left alone with the children and their closest neighbor was a town's distance away.

It seemed like the stories that people had to tell to others became distorted as they traveled from place to place. And why not? If you never would see your neighbor again, how would she confirm or argue about what you said about her?

As technology made communication easier—by phone, mail, and email—the ability to spread gossip increased significantly. You may hear a story about someone that's been told to fifty other people earlier that same morning. And depending on who told you the story, that story could have changed fifty times before it got to you. That story may end up completely different from the original story due to all of the hands it went through along the way.

But most men don't tell stories. Most men don't know how to communicate with each other, let alone spread stories amongst women. It is women that pass along these stories, and some men don't want to deal with them.

In most business circles, it is unprofessional to talk about your personal life. This is business, not some episode of *Days of Our Lives*. When men do business with each other, they may ask about each others' families, but that's as far as it goes. They don't sit there and talk about different emotions or personal problems that they may be going through. This just doesn't happen.

They usually talk about business *and* sports which I've told you earlier are one in the same. I think sports are just a way to talk business secretly without women knowing what they're talking about. When men start talking about sports, what do most women do? They either leave the room, or they tune out the men and start talking amongst themselves. This frees up the men to talk about whatever it is that they want to talk about—and most of the time it's about some form of business. They can disguise this talk in sports terms, and their wives won't get mad at them for bringing home business. It's all very clever.

So why do we all gossip about each other? Could it be jealousy? Could it be because of a feeling of inferiority? Are we just bored? It could be any combination of these things. Sometimes we just don't have anything else to say to each other. Men will refer to sports talk when they don't know what to say to someone. We refer to gossip.

In social settings, that's ok. But in the business world, that doesn't fly. You're here to conduct business and get the job done. No one wants to hear about who did what to whom. I think that's why people that have entry positions often get ignored by upper management. Upper management has enough things to keep them busy during the day. They don't have time for all of the rumors that goes on inside a company. Most people that are in entry level positions find themselves mentally bored with their jobs. These mundane, busy-work-only jobs don't use the creative and unique skills of its associates.

This is why I encourage you to get the training or education necessary to make a move to the next level. This next level will help build self-esteem and will allow you to express your opinions as well as your creativity. It will help develop your character and give you something to be proud of. This is what powerful modern women need to feel that they're making a difference in the world. Use your creativity to move up in your company instead of wasting it in the rumor mill.

Control Your Emotions

Another thing that scares away men in general is an emotion. For some reason, men separate their emotions when it comes to work. If they are having a bad day, they just suck it up and press on until the day is over. We as women aren't programmed that way.

Our emotional side helps to make up our character, and it's very difficult to separate the two. It seems like we're more approachable and open to suggestions than men are. Ladies, think how your men were when you first met them. They were emotionally distanced from you. They seemed to have their guard up twenty-four hours a day, seven days a week. This just seems to be their defense mechanism, and they keep this mechanism alive and well in public too.

Men are very weary of each other and of women altogether. They are always in competition with everyone around them for better positions, authority, and money. Women seem to be more trusting of others and want to incorporate their surroundings into their lives easier than men.

As a powerful modern woman, I've had to find the balance between my female, nurturing side and my hard-core business side. It's taken me seven years and a divorce to be able to separate the two. Hopefully it won't take you the same amount of time to learn your lessons.

Men want women to act like them at work-hard-core, all business, let's get the job done. But they want the softer side when they get home. They want the caring and open person that characterizes our feminine side. And I think that's a good thing.

If we as women want to be successful in the corporate world, we must first put our noses to the grindstone and do business during office hours, and then keep the emotional "drama" for our personal time. You can look at this the same way as sex. Men can separate love and sex. To them it's not the same thing. Love is something you feel towards someone. Sex is a physical action. The two are totally different to men. Just like business and emotions.

Women somewhere through the ages combined the two. We have a hard time separating the emotional side from the physical act. So naturally we would have a hard time separating it at work too. But you must do this if you want men in your environment to view you as an equal.

They see emotions as a weakness. They think that if you show anger or frustration that somehow you're mentally broken. They think that these emotions will cloud your judgment when you need to make a decision about something. It's crazy, I know, but this is what men think.

This is where the term "high maintenance" comes from. A woman that's "high maintenance" is controlled by her emotions as well as her beauty. It's almost like there's no substance there. She's concerned with nothing more than material and frivolous things. And men know this and will treat her accordingly. They will see her as a "trophy" and will treat her with no respect. It's awful, but that's how men are. They believe that "women are too emotional to make logical decisions." And maybe in a way, they're right.

Emotions can cloud our thoughts sometimes. And that's why we have to control them in the workplace. We must be charming and clever, but we can't be dramatic or upset. A powerful modern woman must earn respect from others around her. She can only do that if others in her environment view her as an equal and not a trophy or drama queen.

When men view you as a colleague, your career will start to take a turn for the good. You will find that they trust you and your opinions on different projects. You can't scare them off by being a blabber mouth. You must maintain your composure and in return they will think of you as a professional.

Most people hate going to the dentist. But for some reason they love coming to me. I'm calm, cool, and collected on the outside. But sometimes I get so frustrated or mad that I can't see straight. Usually if something's not being cooperative, I will walk away and gain my composure. No one cares if I'm having a bad day. They just care about themselves and the fact that I get the job done fast and without hurting them. Trust me, it's difficult, but no matter what, I must maintain professionalism at all times. I find that women like me because I'm approachable and nurturing, and I find that men like me because I'm fast, and I get down to business very quickly.

Adapt to Changes

One thing that women can do better than men is to adapt quickly to changes. You could be talking to a young child and then go and take care of a sickly person. Powerful modern women must use this adaptability to their advantage in the business world. You need to be able to "hang out" with the girls but then become "all business" and almost stoic when you deal with the men in your environment.

You must stay very diplomatic in the way you deal with people in your company. You don't want to act snooty with anyone or burn any bridges, because if you become management, your workers will turn against you. You must remain flexible and adapt to the changes in your environment. Remember that men want to do business with you, and women want to be your friend or enemy first. You need to separate the two, and if you can, you'll do great!

In the business world, solutions to problems are created everyday. This is right up a man's alley. Men are used to looking for solutions to daily tasks. By nature, women don't necessarily look for solutions first. We like to analyze problems, the cause of them, the nature of them, and the way they affect our lives. Then we'll try to make the problem go away.

Men want to solve them quickly so they can move onto the next task. They're like zombies taking one step at a time. Women tend to look around and analyze their surroundings and their place in it. We can easily multi-task and get everything done for the day when we put our mind to it. You will need this instinct to survive in the business world.

They will move faster than we will, but we can do more things at the same time; so in the end you can keep up with them. Powerful modern women can adapt to their surroundings and thrive like a beautiful rose plant that blooms all summer long. We just need to be in the right environment and with a little TLC we can grow and prosper in any space.

We've made you aware of "the Perfect Day" and how you can take steps to make your own "Perfect Day" a reality. We've explored what a powerful modern woman is and what it takes to become one. We've explored the business world and how to fit into the male-dominating force that controls it. We've taught you the rules of the business world and how you can adapt your behavior to fit into it. We've discussed some of the reasons why men disconnect with women in the workforce and how we can reconnect with them.

Now we have to talk about why we want to do all of this. What is the impact that powerful modern women have on the world, and why do you want to become one?

Chapter 4

Controlling Assets and Liabilities

In chapter one, we explained what a powerful modern woman is and how to become one. In chapter two, we discussed goal-setting and how easy it is to take the next step in your life. Then in chapter three, we explained the rules of the business world and how to play in it. In this chapter, we're going to explain why playing the correct way in the business world is so important and how to be the winner each and every time!

Earlier we talked about the rules of the business world and how men have manipulated those rules to suit their needs and personalities. Now we are going to explore the psychology of men in the business world and how we as powerful modern women fit into it. With most men, there are three things that they love and they are:

1. sports

2. women

3. beer

Look at it this way; we're in the top three and as a powerful modern woman, you have to use this to your advantage. There's a fine line between using your femininity for good and using it to manipulate people. You need to make sure you're using it to better your position and not to manipulate those around you. Manipulation always has a way of coming back around and kicking you in the butt. It's like that gray hair that you've been fighting against for years. Eventually it always pops out. But how do we use our femininity to our advantage?

Dress the Part

There's many ways to interpret this, but I'll give you the different scenarios, and you can pick the one that you're comfortable with. You can dress to stand out in a good way or in a bad way. If you want to dress to succeed, your wardrobe should be professional. Business suits with either pants or skirts are appropriate. High heels look great, but don't wear them unless you know what you're doing. You must have a confident stride, not look like you're on stilts at the circus. Light makeup—always emphasizing the lips with a great color is important. You want your audience to hear what you're saying, and they'll naturally be drawn to your mouth if your lip color stands out but isn't too bright. Likewise, jewelry is a necessity, but make sure it's complimentary and not chunky. Enhance, don't become a subject for the Fab Five—your dress must exude confidence and show your colleagues that you're confident with your looks as well as your skills.

On the other hand, if you want to have your colleagues talk about you behind your back, go ahead and dress in short skirts, and show off your curves. Or better yet, dress like a complete slob with baggy, bulky sweatshirt material outfits, and see how far you will succeed in your company.

If you find that you're a little overweight to be dressing professionally, and the only thing that fits you is that mumu that is hiding in the back of your closet, let me give you a little advice. Join a health spa or aerobics class, and start to exercise. If you look out of control on the outside, others will think of you as out of control on the inside as well, and will never take you seriously. I'm not the best-looking person in the world, but I look professional when the chips are down. Make sure you're dressing for the occasion. If you're not sure what that is, just ask someone.

Remember, if you look confident, that confidence usually spills over into your personality. Then others will be drawn to you, because they will think you have the answers that they've been looking for. Look the part and you'll find that you fit right in. But please, please, please don't dress like you're a man. In the 1980's, it was "fashion flare" if you wore a man's tie and such, but now it just plain looks tacky. If you dress like a man, you'll just alienate yourself from everyone. Women won't accept you and men won't know what to do with you.

Act the Part

You've learned how to be a powerful modern woman and how to create new goals and objectives for yourself. Now it's your turn to act like it. You look good. People notice you. Now you have to spread your wings and fly. It's all about your confidence level. People won't start to believe in you until you believe in yourself. Remember the saying—"Fake it until you make it." People ask me all of the time—"Wow, you look so young. How long have you been doing this?" In the beginning I'd say "years," because I only had one or two years under my belt, and I didn't think they would feel confident in my abilities. Now I have over seven years of experience, and I figure that this is plenty of time to feel and exude confidence in my skills. You will do the same. Always feel good where your status is right now and feel confident that tomorrow you will be even better. Be patient—I know this is difficult to do, but you must focus on the tiny steps that you are currently making that are bringing your closer and closer to that "Perfect Day."

Times will be difficult; we all know this. Maybe you're a young single woman that's reading this book who just can't make up her mind about what she wants to do with her life. If this is you, then you must take a step back, and look inside your heart, and find out what you really want to do with your life. What kinds of contributions do you want to make to your community and your family/friends? If there's something that you love to do, then there's always a way to make money doing it. Open your mind and follow your thoughts towards the training you need to bring the activity you love to life.

There's nothing holding you back except your own thoughts. Don't act uncertain. You know what you want to do. Even if your family will think you're crazy, don't worry. You'll find out that they'll love you no matter what, as long as you are confident in what you're doing and that you're happy. Be happy—it's not that difficult to do. Live your life the way that you want to live it and the people around you will feel your confidence.

What's the worst that can happen? You fail? Big deal! Failing is not the end of the world. Quitting is! Sometimes you just need to figure out what your Plan B is, and go with it. You'll find in the end that you were put where you were supposed to be.

If you have a family and are ready to again work on your own goals and dreams, you will find that you just need a nudge to get back into the real world. I think it's great that you've sacrificed your dreams to stay at home and take care of your family. But now that the kids are old enough to be in school, it's time for you to work on yourself. How else will your children have role models?

If you have girls, it's your job to set the pace for them to pick up when it's their turn. You must show them that they can have a career and family and that it takes a lot of work but that it's possible to have both.

If you have boys, you must show them that a woman should be treated as an equal contributor to the family and that they must contribute to the household doing things like housework and cooking. If they know how to do chores too, then you're setting up your boys' future to include a loving and long-lasting relationship. Remember that your future daughter-in-laws will be powerful modern women and will not have enough time and energy to have a successful career *and* do all the work at home too. If you bring up a strong man, he will step in and take care of things that she needs help with.

I can't tell you how many men I've dated that didn't know how to cook, clean, or do laundry. I blame their parents for this. My ex-husband didn't cook or clean. He expected me to run a million dollar practice *and* do all the cooking and cleaning. Now I have a man that helps with everything, and it makes things go faster and more smoothly. In my eyes, it's not "women's work" to cook and clean the filth. It's both of our messes; we should both clean them!

Diplomacy

It's tough to be accepted into a new position not only by the new people that you'll be working with but also by the old crowd you're leaving behind. But you need to realize that you're in a very powerful position. You now have friends in both places. You must not alienate anyone! Women on both levels will always come in handy when you need them. Make sure when you're making the transition that you keep the old friends close at hand and don't ignore them after you make the move. Then you must try to fit into the new group too. These women will be your only support system as you battle with the men.

Men tend to stick together, and you must keep your women acquaintances close too. Women will recognize what you're saying and your approach to the problem. A lot of women know what's going on before the men do because of the gossip machine. Keep your ears open but your mouth shut. If you're moving up in the company, you don't want to get mixed up with the gossip, but no one ever said you can't listen to it and make strategic moves that could help promote your position. Sometimes with gossip comes opportunity. Remember the saying that when one door closes, another opens. You can always go back through the previous door. Stay humble, and you'll find that you'll fly under the gossip radar and straight to success!

Even though you must not create waves, you must also stand up for yourself, your skills, and your abilities. Nothing that you do now is ever concrete. Things may need to be changed. Be flexible but firm. We're following the boys' rules of business now, but in the future we'll be rewriting the rules to better accommodate our lives and the way we operate as women. In the meantime there's a fine line between being assertive and being a "bitch." Walk the line but don't go over it, or the derogatory comments will follow. Boy, isn't this fun? I never said being a powerful modern woman was easy, but you're sure to have lots of fun along the way.

When you find that you are moving up in the world—remember that there are other women that want to do the same thing. Utilize other women as much as possible. Go to women for your needs. Doctors, dentists, lawyers, dry cleaners, restaurants, spa owners, hair salons. Any women that you can think of, use them! If we don't use them, who will? Men will go to another man first, and we must do the same. Look up the women business owners in your local phonebook. Also join a women's network. There you will make both professional and personal contacts that may serve you well in the future.

Also help other women out. If you see someone that needs help—give her support. Tell her you understand where she's coming from and that she'll be alright. It's so wonderful to help a fellow sister out and see her succeed. All you need is one person to mentor you, and you can feel high as a kite! Give back to someone. It'll only make both of you feel good!

Sexuality

This is definitely a tricky area. A woman's sexuality can be used to help her in a man's world, but only if she can control it. If she loses that control, men will own her, and her credibility will be shot. When I say sexuality, I don't mean the act of intercourse. When I say sexuality, I mean the manipulation of the senses.

We are in the top three things that men love. Why do they love the other two? We've already discussed why sports are so popular. It's all about being the dominant force—who's the strongest? Who's got the biggest coolios? But why do men like us and beer? Let's take a look at beer.

Men love beer because it's engrained in their blood. From the beginning of time, the barbarians drank malted beverages to celebrate the fact that they were still alive and that they were the top dogs of the area. Beer dulled their senses of taste, touch, and smell and allowed them to get away with pillaging the villages. It was considered very manly to drink malted beverages and tear stuff up.

Even today, it's still considered manly to crack open a Budweiser and socialize with their buddies. To them beer represents heritage, testosterone, and fun. They love the bitterness of the hops. They love the sensation that the carbonation makes on their tongues. This is what men do. They can always find a friend to have a tall cold one with after a hard day's work. To men, beer allows them to feel that the world is good, and they have a place in it.

If beer dulls their senses, then women electrify them. Isn't it amazing that a man could be half asleep, but his head will turn and his eyes will sparkle when a beautiful woman passes in the room? Here lies the difficulty of the subject. How can we as powerful modern women electrify our audience yet not allow them to look at us as just a nice set of legs? I'm not sure there's a concrete answer for this question. I've dealt with it for many years now. I'll give you a couple of examples.

I got into dentistry as you know, as my plan B. I didn't know that "Plan B" really meant "Planet Boys." I stepped right into the boys' club. When I was done with school, I took a job working for a couple of different practices in a suburb of Akron, Ohio. Wow, you'd think Ohio would be out of the dark ages although after re-electing George W. Bush to another term in office, I should have realized that I was involved in the "Club."

Both practices were the same. Men were in charge, and women were doing all the work. I didn't fit in. The women were jealous and temperamental, and the men didn't see me as an equal. I had one dentist that would write me notes on Post-Its and would re-read my treatment notes in the charts and would question my treatment of the patients. I finally shut him up by writing *him* a note on a Post-It telling him to mind his own business. I finally decided to do my own thing and started my own practice. Finally I was the boss and I was in charge. Do you know what I found out? I found out that neither I nor anyone else likes her boss or to be bossed around. No one likes me? The answer was—NO! Luckily I've learned many valuable lessons on the subject I just mentioned earlier.

There's a fine line between using your femininity to get what you want and becoming just another slut sleeping her way to the top. Be careful because sexual harassment can work both ways Like I said, there's always a fine line that must not be crossed when it comes to sex. Office politics are like big soap operas. Sex always comes into play. Don't sleep your way to the top. It's not necessary to have such little respect for yourself and your body. If you let them, men will only use you for pleasure and will never see you as the powerful modern woman that you are inside: as an equal force in the universal. A ying for their yang.

So what's the fine line? You'll know it when you've crossed it. Until you've been burned once, you'll naturally want to play with fire. But once you've been burnt, you never look at fire the same way again. You look at it with a lot less enthusiasm as you did in the beginning.

Be careful of the fire, or as my dad told me—"Don't poo where you eat!" Do not cross the line with a co-worker (especially a married one.) If it's true love, then by all means, you must go for it. But if your "close encounters" are only a play in your sexual chest game to the top, be careful because you'll end up as a pawn chucked to the side of the game instead of being the queen that you deserve to be.

Remember that men are fascinated by women. If they had breasts, they'd never leave their houses. A swivel of the hips and a wink of an eye can get a man excited, and you can warrant some unwanted attention. Friendly is one thing, but you need to watch your flirtatiousness. People will think you're a trouble-maker and will use your manipulation of the senses against you. But this doesn't mean that you have to be strictly 100% business. You can emphasize your femininity without alienating yourself from the pack.

As I mentioned before, the way you present yourself speaks volumes. Men will be more prone to listen to your words than to look at your bosom if you emphasize your lips and not your cleavage. Wear a nice business suit with a skirt once in a while to draw some attention to your nice long legs. But make sure that skirt isn't too short. Leave many things to the imagination. Let those around you know that you're a force to deal with and that you will emphasize your strong points to gain attention as well as respect.

If you can draw men with their eyes, you've won the battle for control. But you must also look non-threatening to other women. You must control them with your words. Women talk. We already mentioned the whole gossip thing. Men love action and seeing objects move. Women are more internal—we have feelings and like to talk about them. We're all into expression. No one likes to be bossed. You must express what you want and need to the women around you without being considered a bitchy boss. Don't boss them; guide them. Make them feel that they can open up with you and that your authority is a protective place for them and their concerns. Remember that you were once in their place. Maybe you'll become a mentor to them and help them make changes in their lives. We never know how someone will react to a certain situation. Control the situation by opening up the men's eyes and opening up the women's ears. You want the boys to see you as powerful, and you want to hear the women around you supporting you and your actions. Without their support, you'll be a dead fish in water.

It's almost as though you'll become a portal to open up communication between men and women. We really do speak a different language. No matter if it's business or personal, we need to make sure that when we communicate with someone that we do it in a way that they will understand. I can have a conversation in Spanish with someone, but if they don't know the language, they won't know what the heck

I'm talking about. This leads us to the next area of discussion which is communication.

Effective Communication

Effective communication can be achieved on many levels and in many ways. You need to read your audience and figure out which method you need to use when you are trying to get your point across to them. There's a big difference between the two sexes on this subject. Men are more visual creatures then women. In general, women tend to understand something if you explain it to her. Still others learn by doing the project, and they learn as they go.

If you are presenting to a crowd, you need to keep these things in mind. The best way to communicate with everyone is to mix the different methods. Visual, auditory, and kinetics (motion) are all equally important to create a dynamic visualization. Most men will be visual, and they want things brief and to a point. If your presentation includes statistics, you can show grafts, pictures, and outline key points. Most men in the crowd can digest this, and you will then get questions from them to explain your key points. To eliminate a lot of questions and to effectively communicate with the women of the audience, you can also explain the key points and tie them in together.

Most women can understand cause and effect relationships. Remember that's what gossip's all about—"Well he did this, and then she did that." Gossip is all about action and consequences. Most women will understand this.

If you're presenting a product, it's best to have a prototype. This prototype can be passed around the room. The men can start to visualize the necessity and logical application of this product. The women can start to comprehend how this product will solve a problem. The people that like to see and hold the product will completely understand the use and practicality of the product and can start to make improvements and think of ways to market the product when they can actually be around this product. It's almost like the product jumped off the pages you're presenting and has sprung to life. A prototype can help to tie all of the methods of communication together.

If your presentation is on a concept only, the more ways your present your information, the more people will understand your concept, and you'll have a higher possibility of success. The following is a brief outline of the things you should present to your audience.

1. Visuals—do you have photos? Grafts? Charts? Limit these to one per slide or per section. If there's too many graphics in front of people, they'll look at the pictures, and they won't listen to you.

2. Auditory—annunciate clearly. Keep your language short and simple. You don't have to use big words to impress your colleagues. Remember that not everyone is as smart as you. That's why you're making the presentation. You want to get as many of these people on your side as possible.

3. Kinetics—(motion). Shift your weight. Smile. Talk with your hands. Fluctuate your voice—high and low as well as soft and loud. If you stimulate your audience with energy, you'll keep their attention.

4. Prototype—give them something to hold and to help demonstrate your points.

If you put these methods together in a presentation, you'll knock everyone's socks off, and you'll be successful in your adventures.

What if you're on a more personal, one-on-one, or in a small crowd? How do you effectively communicate with them? If it's one thing I've learned over the past few years, it's how to talk with someone. It really is easy to read someone's personality. Do they talk in a matter-of-fact way? Are they always joking? Do they want to cut out the small talk and use big words to help shield their insecurity? What do you want from them? Are you trying to get information from them? Are you selling them something?

I think you need to know these things right away. This may be the first time you've ever met this person. If so, be very polite, cordial, and ask questions to try to answer the previous points. Is this person cracking jokes? Is she laughing and talking profusely? If so, these kinds of people will be at ease with you if you do the same. An effective communicator is like a chameleon. They can become part of the crowd once they figure out what the crowd's personality is like.

Is this person shy and quiet? Don't be boisterous with these people. They're introverted and shy. They may need some time to warm up with other people. Give them their space, but you must also be a little aggressive and try to start a conversation with them. If you wait for them to make a move, you may be waiting forever. Don't say too much at one time. You may overwhelm them, and then you'll scare them off. They may think you're too "wild and crazy" for them, and they will shy away from you.

Is this person impatient and huffy? Usually these people are always late, and they seem to be unorganized with their time management. This person won't want to chit-chat with you. They don't have time for gossip—they may be very high strung Type-A personalities. If so, just tell them briefly and simply what you want them to know. Don't ask them too many questions. They may see you as interference to their already-complicated day. Just keep it simple, and then move onto the next person.

Is this person scared or severely intimidated? A little touch on the shoulder or arm can help to relax these types of people. A little physical contact can help assure them that you're not a threat and that you're a warm and caring individual. Speak in lower, softer tones with them and they will naturally be drawn to you. If you can make them feel safe and comfortable, they usually will open up easily to you and will be very loyal colleagues or friends.

These are the main types of people that I've encountered in my business and personal time. Throughout the years, I've learned how to communicate effectively with the different types of people that are out there in the world. This is a very important skill that every powerful modern woman must master if she is to make her presence and her authority known to those in her immediate environment. If you're interested in learning more about effective communication skills, go to my website at www.Thereisnocrying.com and get my book that will be out in 2008, entitled *There's No Crying at Work—A Woman's Guide to Effective Communication.*

Another communication skill that I've found that works on everyone is to bring out her emotions—not yours, but hers. What is it that she wants? There's a difference between what she wants and what she needs. Sometimes it's the same thing, but most people place more value on things that they *want* than what they *need*. They *want* junk food. They *need* to eat healthy. They *want* the Playstation. They *need* to go exercise. See what I mean?

When you have a product or concept that you are presenting to others, you must know how to communicate effectively. You may or may not know the types of personalities that are in the crowd. You may not know if they are men or women or a mixed crowd. But what you need to bank on is that you have something that they want. You may also have something that they need, but if you make them feel the urgency that they want what you have, then you'll sell them every time.

How can you make your product or concept a wish or desire? This takes a little more thought than most methods of communication. This is where a little psychology and a lot of marketing can create the response that you're looking for.

Action

You look the part. You know the lines you must not cross. You know how to effectively communicate with your audience. Now it's time to take action. What's your plan of attack? How are you going to bring the people around you into your fan club? Are you a woman of your word?

In order to become a dominant force in our environment, you must be a woman of action. If you say you're going to do something, do it. When you are sent to a conference to present a new concept or product for your company, you'd better be prepared to blow their socks off. Use your communication skills to capture your audience and convince them that you know what you're talking about.

When you take action, you also build trust. When others trust you to fulfill their needs, they will rely on you. They will know that you will get the job done. If you piddle around, others will know that their project won't get done on time, and they will search for someone else to do it. No, no, no!

You'd better make sure that you're the one that they search for when something needs to get done. Make everything start and stop with you. When you reach this status, you will become very powerful. People will trust you. People will want to work with you. They will rely on you and your skills. This is the spot where you will thrive and build your legacy. Too many people are flaky and unreliable—don't be one of them!

Keep your word! People will respond strongly to you if they know they aren't being misled. If you don't know something, just tell them that you don't know the answer but that you'll find it. They will approach you more often to solve their problems if they know that you're honest with them. You can only fake it for so long. Eventually you're going to have to find out the answers to the questions. You must become an expert in your field, but you can't be a Jill-of-all-trades. There's going to be so many things that you don't know. Don't let this get you down. Learn as much as you can about other subjects. It will only reinforce your power. Knowledge is energy. Use that energy, and learn new skills to increase and replenish it.

Emotions

We've mentioned earlier about controlling your emotions. It's very important to know exactly what emotions we're talking about. Everyone wants to be around others that are polite, intelligent, and encouraging. No one wants to be around a complaining, bitter, nasty person. Make sure you leave your problems at home where they belong. This is business. If you show up and you're in a negative place, you're likely to drag everyone else down there with you. Be courteous and polite with your colleagues and employees. You'll attract more flies with honey than with poo. Make sure that if something isn't working out that you get help from someone that knows what she's doing. Don't be too proud to ask for help. I get flustered all of the time, but I walk away for a few minutes, gather my composure, and jump right back in until the problem is solved. That's the name of the game—hold your temper and frustration for another time.

Don't sweat the small stuff. Don't allow office politics to spoil your mood. I try to avoid them when I can. It comes back to the gossip world that you want to avoid at all costs. Be a mover and shaker, not a gossip maker! Everyone has a bad day—if someone says a snide remark to you-brush it off. Give them the benefit of the doubt. This will keep your environment on a more level playing field. Most men get frustrated and upset at work, but they usually battle through it, because they know their situation is just an obstacle that needs to be worked through.

I encourage positive emotions. If you're passionate about something, show it! When other people see your enthusiasm, they will become enthusiastic too. Positive emotions can be addictive. They can spread like a wild fire through the office. Don't just be a part of the positive vibes; start them! It's so empowering when you project a positive image, and you see others following suit. It makes you feel great, and it helps to get you through those situations where you need a little bit of encouragement.

And speaking of encouragement—give some. Remember that you're going to be moving up the ladder rather quickly, and you will be in a leadership position. Then your main job will be to encourage and empower those around you. Help the women that have helped you advance your career, because they need it too! Sometimes it just takes a little mental support to get someone to change her own life. You could turn into that mentor that we talked about previously. It all comes around full circle. Someone helps you and then later when the time is right, you help someone else. It's a beautiful thing.

Follow Your Instincts

We have so many advantages over men. But we must know how to tap into those assets if we are to dominate and control our environment. One asset that all women have is to multi-task. We can work on multiple things at the same time and get everything done at once. Men can't do that. Men always have blinders on and don't look around them long enough to see that they could be doing something else while they're waiting for something to get done.

Women always know what's going on and can manage to break down their actions into sequential steps. We can stop the process at any point, do something else, and then come back and start that same project where we left off. We understand the process of getting to the end of the project better than men do. I'm not sure if this is an instinct or a learned behavior that our mothers taught us as little girls. But however we received this skill, it doesn't matter. Multi-tasking is a very important skill to have, especially as you advance through your career.

If you're in management or are a business owner, if you can't multi-task, you're a dead duck in the water. In managerial positions, you're playing the chess game. You know your objective and the number of steps it will take to get there. You then must move your team of pawns in different positions until the objective is met. If you can't see the big picture and how things are supposed to be done, you won't be able to solve all of the obstacles or counter moves that will get in your way during the process.

If you can walk and chew gum at the same time, then you're a multi-tasker. If you can take care of the kids, cook dinner, and sort through the mail all at the same time, you're definitely qualified. Take this wonderful skill and use it to your advantage. Others will notice how efficiently and quickly you get things done when you can put all of your resources to work together at once!

Another instinct that women have is our sixth sense. Somehow we've been blessed with that feeling that something's the matter. Somewhere in the universe, something's not right. If you tap into that feeling, it will help guide you through different obstacles into greener pastures. That sixth sense can lead you out of turmoil, or it can also make you expand your thoughts on a certain subject.

This instinct may lead you to insights on a different way around a problem. Sometimes you need to think out of the box. That funny little feeling in the pit of your stomach can help keep you out of trouble if you listen to it. If it doesn't feel right, don't do it. That's what the sixth sense is. It's your self-conscience talking to you. Every woman has it but some women listen to it more than others.

But don't confuse the cautiousness of your sixth sense with fear. If you're afraid to do something because of failure or self-doubt, this is different than the sixth sense. The only thing that the sixth sense does is to make you stop and think about the consequences of an action that will take place. That's all! It's a checkpoint to the mind that bridges thoughts to actions. This is a positive thing that can be thought of as self-protection. Fear and negative self-doubt are something completely different and are things that need to stay out of your life for good. But your sixth sense can help you make important decisions and can keep your life on the right track.

Another instinct that you have is to organize not only your thoughts but also your environment into a logical order. If you've ever moved, you get to your new place and something takes over you that tell you where to put all of the stuff. This is your organizational gene that's coming to the surface: The dishes go here. The tissues go there. Even though this is a natural instinct for women, some of us are better at utilizing this skill than others. The ones that are great at this are also great event planners and managers, because they can not only organize their own thoughts into some sort of order, but they can also organize physical objects too. Keeping things in order helps to keep your life on track.

Too many times we allow clutter into our lives-either thoughts that aren't important or worse yet, negative thoughts and people—to enter into our environment. Clutter usually brings chaos. Chaos brings negativity. This can be a main obstacle. If your environment's a mess, your life probably is too. Don't be a pack rat. Leave your emotional as well as your physical junk/baggage at the curb. You don't need it anymore. There are so many people that are worse off than you are emotionally and physically. Get rid of the junk in your life and organize it the way you want it to be. Powerful modern women take control of their lives, and using their organizational skills can help to do this.

Another instinct we all have is as a natural nurturer. Most of us will be mothers at some point in our lives. As a mother, your comforting instinct kicks in. You want to protect and comfort your children throughout their lives. This instinct can be used in the business environment also. Everyone has a bad day or gets hung up on a certain project. A leader recognizes this and helps that person through the problem.

If you get into a management position or you own your own business, you will have problems thrown at you all of the time. Sometimes the only thing you can do is to comfort another person until the solution to the problem becomes clear. This is a great instinct to use. If you can hold your temper and disappointment back and use your positive, nurturing side, you'll find that communication will become easier no matter whom you're talking to. This can also be reciprocated. As women, sometimes we just need a shoulder to cry on, not necessarily a solution to the problem. If you help someone when she is in need, maybe in the future you will find someone to help you in return. Give a little, and you will receive so much more. Don't ignore this special skill.

The last instinct I want you to tap into relates to listening. Women are naturally great communicators. I don't know how women survived before telephones. I love to call my girlfriends up and gab about things for hours. And as women, we need to not only communicate effectively, but we must also listen effectively. Sometimes people will be upset about something on the outside but will have an entirely different issue on the inside. As an effective listener you can blow through the smoke screens and get to the real problem. This helps during presentations or if you're trying to sell something.

I sell dental services—that's what dentists do. We have hundreds of skills that we know how to do, but we need to sell those services to people. Most of the time, it's an easy sell because either they're in pain or they look awful and can't function normally. Once in awhile, I'll have a difficult sell ahead of me. I always listen to what they are interested in doing, and then I give my presentation. I tell them the pros and cons of doing the procedure and any other procedures that can be done in substitution for the mentioned procedure. Then I shut up, and I listen to them. If they give me any excuses like, "I can't afford it right now," or "I'll have to talk to my spouse about it," I have enough experience in the business world that I can see right through those excuses.

I look out of my window into the parking lot and can see what kind of car they drive. I can also see their clothes, make-up, cell phone, and other accessories and can tell you what their excuses really are. If they have the nice clothes, the nice car, and the cell phone, then my services aren't wanted yet. My services aren't high on their priority list like their other possessions. I then try to make them an emotional offer by offering them something that I know that they would like—payment plans, free whitening, whatever to try to make it an emotional, gotta-have-it thing.

Most of the time this works, because then they see that they really do want my services and may even need them and that they're getting something that can change their self-esteem and self-image forever. If they still don't see the need or want for my services, then I step back and end the conversation with an encouragement to come see me when they are ready. Usually when I see them again, they've thought about things and have decided to go through with my services.

Being able to listen effectively has nothing to do with your ability to hear them. You must also understand their words and the situation that they are coming from. Most of the time, you can then determine what the real problem is, and you can either solve it, or be there to support them. It's amazing what you can find out about someone if you take the time to learn a little about them and their present situation. If you ask them what they want, most of the time they will tell you. If you assume you know what they want, you'll be wrong every time. Don't assume. If you break down the word it tells you exactly what it means ...

"ASS" out of "U" and "ME"= ASSUME

Don't assume anything. If you want information, just ask. If you ask a direct question, nine times out of ten, you'll get a direct answer. Don't be like a man driving—he will turn down every wrong road there is before he goes to a gas station and asks for directions. Why? That's one of the great mysteries of the world. I don't want you to wonder around the universe—ask the questions; then shut up, and listen to the answers. Sometimes you'll get direct answers, and sometimes you'll need to interpret the answers; then you'll need to ask more questions to get the information you really want. But you need to shut up and listen to get the information that you want.

Be Resourceful

One of the best things you have going for you as a woman is being creative and resourceful. Unlike a man, you have the ability to take off your blinders and see the world around you. We may not like change, but it's easier for us to adapt to the changes around us than it is for men.

We seem to be in-tune with our bodies, our feelings, and our environments. This is a good thing! Use this towards your advantage. Let's say that you've found out that there's a major problem with a deadline on a project that you are working on. Let's say that your department needs to do certain parts of the project, and there are two other departments working on it also. Why do you have to go in order or have just one department work on things at a time? Why can't you either work on things out of order and finish everything on time, or work on the parts simultaneously to get it done all at once? This is just an example of working through problems.

You have to "think out of the box" if you're going to help fix every day problems. Maybe your supervisor hasn't thought of the most obvious way to solve the issue. Gently approach him/her and give your thoughts. Especially if you're in a management position, you must use the resources around you (your team) to finish the project and be ready to move onto the next one.

When you have lunch with fellow colleagues, make sure that you know what they do and what department they work for. You never know when you may need to make a phone call and ask one of them for an unexpected favor. It's always easier to work with someone you know and like than to work with a complete stranger.

If you do have lunch with colleagues, make sure these are not just social lunches but also networking lunches. These people may need you to come to their rescue in the future. These lunches can also lead to other projects that may come up in the future. Wouldn't it be cool to work with your friends as much as possible? Look out for each other, and help one another as much as possible.

You have to remember that there are only so many ideas out there. That's why Hollywood is having such a hard time making movies—there's only so many ideas for them that most of them have already been done. So you must use your creativity and originality to help solve the problems in the world today. Think of the technology that's out there. Twenty years ago they couldn't have imagined the

internet and all of the information that you can get from it. It's a wonder how I made it through college in the early 90's without the internet. I know I've gained a lot of knowledge from the internet. There are
so many different speakers out there that know different business skills
such as website design and cash flow management that this book
wouldn't have been possible if the internet wasn't around.

The internet is an easy way to learn new skills too. You can learn
how to do different things like wire a ceiling fan—I just did that two
nights ago—or even learn how to cook your favorite recipe. There are
so many things you can learn on the web that it's crazy. When a problem at work arises, look for solutions on the web. Maybe there's a book
written about your certain subject, or maybe there's a company out
there that does exactly what you need. The information that you need
is just a click away. Make sure that you know how to use the computer
and the internet. If you don't know how to use the technology, either
ask your ten year old—he/she probably knows more than most adults
out there—or take a computer class at your local library or community
college.

There are so many people out there that have unique skills, and the
internet is an easy way to find them. If you are hiring someone for a
particular position in your company, the internet features different
sites with people looking for jobs. Maybe you want to learn how to
increase the traffic to your website or to your business; there's a lot of
information of the web for this. This is where I got my information to
write this book. I had never heard of publishing a book myself, I got a
couple of books on it, attended a couple of seminars, and here I am.

I've learned over the years that I'm just "practicing." That's why
they call my business a practice. Everyday I see unique and different
situations, and I have to adapt my skills that I've learned over the years
to try to solve that problem. Everyday I learn something new. A different technique or a different way to approach a problem whether it
involves dentistry or people in general. And this is a good thing. Pow-

erful modern women never settle. They always improve themselves and take each step in stride.

I owe a lot of my self-improvement to the internet. I've met so many new people that I may never have known if it wasn't for the internet. I've learned how to build a website—which I hated, and I learned how to market it effectively in my practice.

When I got out of school, I was burnt out. I was in college for eight years and swore up and down that I would never read another book again. After six months of following my convictions, I picked up a dental journal and learned about a new product that shaved off half of my time when I did a certain kind of filling. After that I was hooked. I now get ten journals, four newsletters, and have a monthly marketing coach that I listen to. I've come to realize that I am a professional student, and I will always have the curiosity of a cat. I will never stop learning new skills as long as I live. I think that's a good philosophy to live by. If you're always learning and improving yourself, you will feel as though you're living your life. If you're content in your everyday atmosphere, you will find that you feel like you're dying inside. And you are. That's your child curiosity that's dying. But if you get yourself into adventures, you will find that your will be full of life and vigor!

Educate yourself on different subjects. You never know when you might need that information. Remember that knowledge is power and no one can take that away from you. You may never need that knowledge, but wouldn't you rather know that you have it stored in the depths of your brain? It's like insurance. You never know when you may need it. Sometimes you will, and sometimes you won't, but in the back of your mind you'll always know it's there if you need it. Make sure you stay up with the times as in technology and current trends. If you're a buyer for a company, this is very important. There are always trends that need to be followed and changed. The internet is an easy way to follow these trends so that you can make your decisions when the time is right.

Always keep your options open. Never cancel out any of the possibilities—you just never know how things will turn out. Keep your friends close and your enemies closer. You never know when you may need someone to do a favor for you. Be the one who keeps in communication with your friends and associates. Invite someone to lunch or to a BBQ at your house sometime. I know we're all very busy with our own families, but think of someone else for a change. Maybe someone is going through a rough time and doesn't have anyone to reach out to. Maybe you could be that person.

Don't have a bad attitude about this. I know this takes some effort on your part, but that's all that it is—it's a little effort. Be the initiator. You will do much better after you've talked to that friend you haven't been in touch with for ages. It's good for your psyche, and you will make her feel great also. I'm the aggressor with most of my friends. I usually am the one that does the calling. For some reason, they are too busy with their own lives to ask me what's going on with mine. I don't like that. I want to know what's going on with my friends. I want to make sure everything's ok and that I can reminisce with them about the good ol' days.

Even if you've just met someone new, reach out to them. Maybe they're new in the neighborhood, and they don't know anyone. My neighborhood is a new development and from day one, we have monthly ladies' nights where anyone can come to the hostess's house for a themed social hour. I, of course, was the first one to hold a social night, and I've had one every year since. It's an easy way to get in touch with some people from the neighborhood whom I haven't seen for a long time, and I also meet new people. I always use it for social purposes as well as a chance for a networking opportunity. New neighbors equal an opportunity for new business. Almost everyone that comes to my social events has become patients over the years. See, what did I tell you? It requires you to make up an invitation, buy some munchies, and clean up your house. That's it! But the rewards far outweigh the costs! Try it sometime! I know you'll have fun.

Most people are lazy. Powerful modern women are nothing but lazy! This goes hand in hand with self—improvement and being resourceful. I know it's so easy to be content in your own little world with no friends or events on the social calendar. Phooey! That's not the way to live. Spice things up a bit. Go on some adventures! Do you want to learn some cooking skills? What about how to scrapbook? If you have a hobby you'd like to pursue, today's society is jam-packed with events and clubs that you can join to learn and enjoy different hobbies.

Are you into golf or tennis? Join a league with some friends or join by yourself, and open your mind to meeting new people. You never know what new contact is out there. Maybe you've been working on a new set of skills, and it's time to move up the corporate ladder. These clubs and social settings can be a great place to make contacts that could land you an interview for that new job that you're looking for. Men have been using the golf excuse for years. Most people are lousy golfers—I know because I am—and they just go out on the course to do business, have a few drinks, and enjoy the weather without distractions. Wow, what an excuse! You need to do that too!

Relaxation/Stress Relief

To be resourceful, you need to be creative. To be creative, you need to be well-rested. This includes getting enough sleep and also relaxing your mind. I know our days are hectic with work and with family issues that are always springing up, but if you don't take some time for yourself, you'll have a nervous breakdown!

One of the easiest and most relaxing things that you can do is to take a bubble bath. In today's busy world, we usually take a quick shower and then finish getting ready to go. Not a lot of people take the time to take a nice hot bubble bath. I have a jet tub and I try to take at least one bubble bath a week. This is a good example of a way to relieve some of your daily stress.

There are many reasons why a hot bubble bath is a great stress reliever. Heat relaxes muscles. Most of the time you will spend at least thirty minutes in a tub full of hot water. This will expand the muscles and will allow all of the built-up toxins to be released from the body. Many athletes use this technique as part of their training technique.

Using some type of bubble bath product helps to moisturize the skin. During the day, the skin is exposed to different harsh elements of the environment that dry out the skin. This includes changes in temperature and pollution. These elements can make the skin itchy and chaffed. Allowing the skin to soak in the bubble bath products that contain many oils, the skin can then rehydrate and rejuvenate.

The aromas in the bubble bath products also help to relax the muscles. The water vapor from the hot water releases these aromas and can relax nasal tissues that can make you breathe easier. You can shut the door and get the quiet time that you need. Keep the kids and the spouse out of your space! This is the best excuse you can have to have some "me" time! Put the kids to bed and take thirty minutes to take a bubble bath.

Our lives are congested enough. We need to take time out to revitalize our mind, body, and soul. Follow the steps below to help relieve the daily stress that always seems to creep up on us when we least expect it.

1. Avoid Loud Sounds. Loud sounds can cause the body to be in an over-stimulated state. This can make all of your senses "on-edge" and make you more susceptible to stress. Meditation is a great way to relax your mind. It all starts with focusing your mind on your breathing rate. If you can take five minutes in a quiet part of your office, you can refocus your mind on the tasks ahead of you. You can close your eyes and concentrate on your breathing. Slowly breathe in through your nose and then slowly out through your mouth. Repeat this until your breathing rate slows down. When you're done, you'll notice that you will feel revived and more relaxed.

2. Listen to Soft Music. Another relaxation method is by listening to soft quiet music—No heavy metal or punk rock here! A smooth jazz or love song station will do the trick. One of the worst times to be stressed out is during the drive home. Traffic is always bad, and if you have a long commute home, you will have plenty of time to build up a high stress level that will be taken out on your family or friends. But tuning into a soft, smooth music station, you will hear methodic, soft melodies that will naturally quiet your mind and relax your senses that have been in over-drive since the start of your day. Your mind will feel refreshed when you get home. Your family will thank you.

3. Exercise! You need to not only relax your mind but your body too. Exercise is the best stress reliever there is. If you're new to exercise (you haven't done it since the 70's,) then now is the time to start doing something. Join a gym, hire a personal trainer who will look over your physique and develop a specific plan for you.

If you exercise once in a while, now is the best time to get yourself in a more consistent regimen. Consistent exercise even if it's only a thirty minute walk once a day will help to not only burn extra calories that you've eaten during the day, but it will also keep your insulin levels stable which is a main factor of obesity.

4. Food. You have to have a balance in the types of food that you consume everyday. You must eat the proper amounts of fats, carbohydrates, and proteins. I understand that it's not practical to eat strictly every day. I think it's more of a mental game than a physical craving, but you need to eat properly six out of the seven days a week. Give yourself a break on that seventh day. Eat like a hog! Eat whatever you want. If you want pizza or a burger, go for it! You're body will forgive you. It's important to live your life. Make food fun, but make sure you give your body what it needs.

Certain foods like Chamomile tea, warm milk, and chocolate can cause a state of relaxation. Treat yourself to one of these treats after a long day's work. You'll find that these foods will relax your mind as well as your body.

5. Frequency. Eat often. It's recommended that you eat at least five times a day with three main meals and two snacks. When you eat less food and more often, your body can easily digest the food that you consume. Your metabolism will stay on track, because there's constant food in the stomach to digest. But make sure these meals and snacks are healthy and balanced.

6. Stretch. It's not good for your body to be in the same position or to do repetitive motions all day long. Muscles can easily fatigue, and this can cause headaches and cramping. Take a break and stretch. This helps to stretch the muscles which can relieve any pressure that are placed on joints and nerves. Yoga is a great way to stretch the body and also to strengthen it.

7. Moisturize. This includes inside and out. Our environment can cause dry skin and also internal dehydration. Keep skin moisturized and drink plenty of water to keep you energized!

8. Date night. Intimate time with your significant other is very important to relieve stress. It's a time to reconnect and to discuss issues that need to be taken care of. With kids and work it always seems like everyone else has a little piece of you, and your relationship suffers. Don't let this happen to you!

Date night—this is very important. There's thousands of babysitters out there—use one! Set aside one night a week or every other week, and take your lover out for the evening. I don't care if it's only for dinner or a movie. Remember when you were dating how good you felt after the date? You were electrified and felt on a "high" for at least a week. Even though you're now a "ball and chain" this feeling doesn't have to end. Try a new place to eat, or try a new activity that you've always wanted to do but never made the time to do it. No matter what it is, at least you're spending time with the most important person in your life.

9. Intimate time. Make sure you are setting a certain amount of time aside for intimacy. Too many marriages end because there's not enough time spent in this area. Yes, we're all tired after fighting with work and the kids and the housework and all of the other things that fill the hours of our day. But hey, you need a little attention too! And if you need it, you'd be assured that your partner needs it too. Get out of those baggy clothes and put on something sexy. It'll make you feel good and your partner feel as though he really matters to you. Keep the connection both physically and mentally going. Your relationship depends on it!

10. Humor. Stop being so serious all of the time. It's just stressing you out. No one can live her life not having fun. Go tell a joke. Humor is an essential part of life. Not only can it stop a fight in its tracks, it can strengthen your stomach muscles too! What a great benefit!

Go watch a sitcom or a comedy movie. Learn a joke. There's a lot of joke-a-day websites on the internet that will send you a joke everyday. This can start your day off on the right track. It also opens up the lines of communication with your family, friends, and coworkers. Humor is a lot like pizza. Both are universal. Everyone has heard of both and can relate to both. Most people love pizza and they will love you too if you have a good joke to tell them once in awhile.

If you need to communicate with someone, you'll find that if you add a little humor to the conversation that it goes a lot smoother. You'll become more approachable if you use humor as your main defense weapon and not anger or aggression. It takes more facial muscles to frown than to smile!

Make Something Happen

Stress is a normal thing in both the business and personal world. But you still have to take care of yourself. If you want to move up the corporate ladder or take that new pottery class you've had your eye on, you need your strength also. This requires you to do what all of the physicians in the world have been saying for decades—eat right, exercise, and get some rest! No one said you had to be superwoman! But you will have to step out of your normal world, and pick up the pace at least one notch if you're going to see any progress.

Don't be lazy! I know we all get tired and we just want to sit around and watch TV and become couch potatoes. But nothing is going to change in your life if you do this. This is probably what you've already been doing for the past few years. You've probably put on a few pounds and have been feeling lousy. I'm here to tell you now to stop that! Make something happen. You owe it to all of the women who have struggled in the past to get up off your butt, and make a contribution to society. You also owe it to all of the future generations to come. Who better than yourself to show them the way: To show them that they can do whatever it is that they want to do with their lives with just a little bit of effort? I know you can do it!

Remember that insanity is doing the same thing over and over again expecting a different result. If you want changes in your life, you must do something that's different from your normal routine. Throughout this book, I've gone over many examples of how to make these changes. I've taught you how to identify change and how to set goals for yourself to see that change through. I've also taught you how to play the boys' game, especially in the business world.

It's very important to play the game, but how could you play before without knowing what the rules were? I've also given you different strategies to help bring your career into the successful mode. But everything starts with some effort on your part. You must want to change. I can't do it for you. You must love yourself and your children enough that you want to go and make a contribution to society. That's how civilization changes and improves. Without people like you and me, we'd stay stagnant and would never know what it was like to feel alive.

When you decide that you want to make some kind of change in your life, you will start to feel more energized. That's your child curiosity coming alive again. Some of us lose that curiosity as we get busy with everyday life. Don't let this happen to you! This curiosity is the main energy source that helps to drive you to do the things that must get done if you are to change your environment.

Make the curiosity come alive, and get rid of the drama! If you're around negativity all of the time, you will feel stressed out, and your curiosity energy will slowly whittle away. If you're in a dead-end job, if you're struggling with your finances, if your relationship is going down the drain, this is the perfect time to stop, look around your environment and write down the changes that you want to make. When you stop to smell the roses, you discover things that you may not have noticed before.

Some of those things may be right in front of your nose but you were so busy doing the everyday mundane things that you probably didn't notice that they even existed. This is usually how our slumps begin. We become numb to our environment that we don't notice that anything is changing for the good. We need to stop this method of going through the paces, and do something constructive.

Recently I read an article that said that we as Americans spend between four and six hours a day watching television. Holy cow! No wonder we made so much progress in the 1800's—we didn't have television sets to waste our time. We need to stop this! Get outside. Go meet some people. Do something fun and fulfilling! You will feel so much better about yourself and your situation if you've made some kind of stride towards improving your environment.

I know things may be difficult. You may be in hard times. But this is no excuse. I don't care if your steps are baby steps, go out and do something. If you're in a bad relationship—get out of it! I struggled for three years in a loveless marriage that did nothing for my ego or my emotional side. But I too was afraid of doing things on my own—yes, even I was afraid to make a move towards my independence. But when my marriage was on the rocks, I took that extra time that I had and started to work on my business and my own improvement. I started to exercise. I started to study nutrition. I started to learn about the internet and how to market effectively on it. I started to read some philosophy and some spiritual writings on the web. All of this allowed me to have the strength to get through the life-changing time that I faced after my marriage ended.

I took the time to work on myself. I took the time and put the energy to make sure that after things were all said and done, that I would have learned a valuable lesson and would be a better person for it. I started to laugh more. I started to get rid of all of the negativity and drama in my life. I started to breathe easily again. I haven't been this happy since college. I also promised myself that I would never allow negativity to rule my life again and that I would do whatever it took to live a happy life. And ever since then, I've been a better person for it. My business is thriving to the point where I can finally pay off my student and business loans and my personal life is filling my heart with adventure and happiness.

Most people don't realize that most doctors, lawyers, dentists, or any other small business owners have to borrow extreme amounts of money to not only go through school but also to start their own businesses. And there's no guarantee that things will work out for you either. You just have to take a leap of faith and believe in yourself and the skills that your school taught you. That's all that you have to go by.

And of course, you have to study the rules of business and follow your instincts. So the next time you go to a small business and complain about your bill being too high, remember the sacrifices that this person made and appreciate the fact that she/he had the courage to learn their craft and bring it to you to enjoy. Until you take a step in their shoes, you have no clue what type of sacrifices they made to be in the position that they're in right now. And they deserve the price that they're asking to deliver their service to you!

So stop complaining about your life, and go find a way out of your current situation. No one likes a whiner. No one likes to be around someone who is negative all of the time. Believe in yourself, and find a mentor to help you. Go back to school. Decide where you want your life to be in the next month. If you start planning for the future, you'll find that the steps will be easier to follow than to go about life blindly.

They say that if you fail to plan, you plan to fail. I think that this is only half of the truth. I don't think that anyone is a failure. But I do think that you won't be successful in your own mind if you don't plan to succeed. And succeeding always takes self-improvement. So go out and start to do something different.

Apply for that new job that has opened up in your company. Go back to school to finish that degree you never finished. Start a study club to meet other business owners that are interested in joint marketing ventures. I don't care what it is that you do, but you do have to put some thought into your direction, and then you must take some action towards that path. It sounds a lot harder than it is. If you want to get back into shape after having children, grab the stroller and take a walk. Anything you do will be a step in the right direction.

Make sure that you find some kind of support system. Whether it's a trainer, a mentor, or a spouse, we all need encouragement along the road to change. A mentor is the best thing you can have to help guide you to your next step. If you follow the path that someone else has already traveled, the journey becomes so much easier than if you go it alone. You don't have to reinvent the wheel here. Find someone that is doing the exact thing that you want to be doing, and get in touch with her. She will be honest and sincere in her guidance, and you will make a friend in the process.

Then when it's your turn, you can pass on your knowledge and experience to another woman that's in the same situation that you were in. It's a great cycle to become part of. To learn the ins and outs of an obstacle, to overcome it, and then to lend a helping hand to someone else is truly a beautiful thing.

You've learned how to act in the business world. You've gained the tools and the traits needed to be a powerful modern woman. You've learned how to interact with your environment and those around you. Now you need to learn how to put everything else in your life in order so that you can focus your efforts on succeeding in your career field.

Chapter 5

Priorities

To help you get started in your adventures that lie ahead of you, you must be able to put things into perspective. This includes categorizing your life into priorities. You need to sort through people, relationships, and objects and see what things are important and what things aren't. You can't focus on your career if your personal life is full of chaos. Powerful modern women don't allow clutter to bog them down. They invite change and know that they will have to clean out their closets now and then to be able to have the freedom to move onto the next step.

Clean Out the Closets

To get started, you need to become organized. We talked earlier about getting rid of the clutter around you. I've seen many people that live in complete filth. It's ok to have bills and papers on your desk once in awhile but to live that way all of the time is not going to work. Tell the kids and your spouse to get off their butts and start organizing things. Start with their closets—at least twice a year, make your family go through her/his closets and get rid of anything that doesn't fit or that she/he hasn't worn for at least one year. Throw them all in a bag and give them to Goodwill or the Salvation Army.

Then you can start on the rest of your house. After my divorce, I realized that most of the clutter that was in my house wasn't from me. It was from my ex-husband. He was a clutter freak. He used to save everything. When we were sorting through things—I should say when

I sorted through things, I found old knobs and wires, old pieces of pipe, and old knick knacks from our previous house. I put all of that stuff in a pile in the garage and let him pick and chose what he wanted, and then the rest I threw out. Do you know that he picked up every little piece of scrap metal and knobs? He doesn't even know what a screw driver is but he had to have all of this stuff. I'm not sure if the clutter made him feel safe or important or what, but believe me, you don't need it.

Clutter won't make your life any easier; it will only stir up chaos. Have you ever lost your keys because you didn't put them where they were supposed to go, and then you found them in the pile of papers that you never threw away? It took you longer to sort through the clutter to find your keys than it did to throw the clutter out! Do me and you a favor and throw the clutter out! You don't need it. If you haven't used that scrap wood that's been sitting in your garage for three years, guess what? You never will! Throw it out. You can always get more if you need it in the future, which is highly doubtful. Throw it out! Or recycle it. Or give it to your local school that has a woodshop. They're always looking for donations for the kids.

Go through your old bills and tax papers and throw out the old ones. Warranties and other important papers should be put in a separate folder, and old ones should be shredded and thrown out. Go to the store and buy one of those file cabinets. You can put them in a closet out of sight. Get some folders and go through all of your papers and organize them. This is a good winter project or something for the kids to help you with. If it's a big project, just do a little at a time. Rome wasn't built in a day. Chip away at it a little at a time: You will find that by the end of the week that it'll all be done, and you'll be able to move onto the next adventure.

Finances

This is a very important issue that you have to be comfortable with if you want to be successful and have the life that you've always dreamt of. When you are setting goals for your life, you need to make sure that financial goals are part of your system. Without money, the chances of you living a long prosperous life are very low. I'm not saying that you have to be a greedy woman, but you have to be a little frugal in your everyday life, and you need to prioritize your spending habits.

The first thing you must learn to do is to live within your means. My grandparents were wonderful role models for this. One set of grandparents lived within their means and saved money whenever they had a chance. They ended up retiring early and moved to Florida. They bought different properties, fixed them up and sold them for a profit. That profit is what they now live on and invest with. They bought all of their possessions in cash and don't believe in getting things that they can't pay for in cash. This way of living has greatly influenced my family and the way I live my life today.

My other set of grandparents worked really hard all of their lives, but apparently spent what they earned. When my grandfather was forced to retire early from his job, he went on a pension. Now that they have social security, they use that money and what little is left from his pension. I feel very sad for them, because they were always so loving to me. To see them struggle with medications and cars is not very fair to them. But that's how the cookie crumbles if you don't start to save now.

If your company has a retirement plan, you need to sign up with it immediately. Talk to a financial advisor about how important compound interest is in growing your savings for your elder years and what kind of plan is within your means. Most companies will match part of your salary at the end of the year, but if you don't even sign up for the plan, you're throwing away money that could be in your pocket when you're older.

Credit cards are the root of all evil. If you are swamped in credit card debt, now is the best time to start to climb your way out of it. Oprah had a bunch of shows on how to climb out of debt. If you want more information on steps you can take to pay them off early, check out her website at www.oprah.com.

Why do you charge things on credit cards? Are you trying to keep up with the Joneses? Do you think that material things will make you feel safe or more important? I hate to be the one to tell you this, but they won't! If you don't have the money now to pay cash for it, why do you think that you'll have the money to pay for it later? When you see the kind of interest that you're paying for these items, you may want to think again before you decide to charge them.

I hear the same thing all of the time in my office—"I can't afford to fix my mouth." Usually when I hear these words, I hear it coming from people that may not have a lot of money but walk around in expensive designer clothes and have a nice car and the newest cell phone. Ok people, where are your priorities? Maybe you don't have a lot of money, but your health will last you a lot longer than any of those material things. You must focus on what your priorities are in life: Sort through them, and get rid of the stuff that won't get you that next job.

Do you want to put your kids through college? I know what college cost me, and ten years later I'm still paying for it. If you want them to have a successful financial life, you must teach them to live a little more frugally. Does anyone need twenty pairs of jeans? Thirty pairs of shoes? Cable with ten movie stations? Take out your checkbook sometime, and see where your money is going? Are you getting gourmet coffee everyday for three dollars? Do you eat out all of the time? You could cut that out, and put that extra cash on your credit cards to pay them off. Or you could put that extra money into a savings account for yourself or your family for future use.

Did I say savings? Yeah! Most of the people I talk to everyday only have a few hundred dollars in a savings account. It still surprises me to this day. What do you do if something major happens? What if your car's transmission goes out? Insurance will only pay for so much, and if you don't have a rental car on your plan, you may have a transportation problem on your hands. What happens if one of your children breaks his/her leg? Medical bills can be expensive even with insurance. Taking time off work can create havoc on your wallet. If you had a small nest egg to go to in times of need, you wouldn't feel the stress that these situations put you in.

If I learned anything from my grandparents, I learned that you have to live within your means and save for a rainy day. From the first time that I started working, I took ten percent out of each paycheck and put it away into savings. I have enough of a savings now that I just remodeled my basement without having to take out a home—improvement loan and still can pay my bills for six months if something were to happen to my health. If you save a little money on a consistent level, you will always live in abundance.

Start to prioritize your money. You need to make your savings and retirement contributions first and then pay your bills. After that, you can spend whatever is there. If you can do this, you should be out of debt and on your way to being financially free. But it does take discipline. And you have to be frugal.

You must learn how to cook. It's not brain science. Start watching the Food Network. I've learned so much from watching the different chefs on that channel. It's helped me to get away from fatty junk food that most restaurants serve and onto more healthy veggies and fresh meat. I now would rather spend money at the grocery store knowing that I am in control of what I put inside of my body than to trust some cook that doesn't care about my health. And it's a lot cheaper too. With all of the money that you save from paying someone else to prepare your food, you can pay off credit cards or save for that new furniture that you've had your eye on.

Education

Maybe your priority is to go back to school to help finish your degree and get a new job. I know how expensive school can be, but there are many ways to pay for it. If you can be more frugal with your everyday spending, you will find that you will have enough money at the end of the month to pay for a college class. You may need to work and take one or two classes at a time at night to finish your degree, but who cares? A degree is a degree. It doesn't matter how you got it. It only matters that you got it. And once you have it no one can take it away from you, and you can keep building your portfolio for future jobs.

You can also take out student loans, get a state grant, or even a scholarship. If you're worried about the financial aspect of going back to school, there are so many plans out there to help you get on track. Call the college financial office and discuss your options. Also look on the internet for federal and state financial programs, many of which are grants and do not have to be paid back.

If you want to start your own business, the Small Business Association (SBA) is a wonderful resource to use if you're looking for financial advice. There are loans and contacts that the association can hook you up with to help you get your business up and running. If you need to write a business plan to apply for a loan, either the SBA or the federal government can help you write up the plan. Go to www.Firstgov.com for instructions on how to write up a business plan, how to hire employees, and how to market your business. All of this is free information waiting there for you to use.

Remember that a mentor is an invaluable resource to help you spread your wings and get off the ground. Whether it's to learn new skills for a new position to opening up your own business, a mentor can help lead you to financial success. If she is doing what you want to do, ask her questions and follow her advice. It's easier to go down a road that's been traveled than to draw the map on your own!

Relationships

Here's a tricky subject. You need to get all of the drama out of your life so that you can concentrate on your and your family's futures. You can't do this if your life is filled with negativity. If your relationship with your significant other includes drama that is keeping you from succeeding in life, then you must end that relationship! It's your life!

You must live it the way that you want to live. If your spouse doesn't support you in your new steps towards financial freedom and career success, then your spouse doesn't love you. Your spouse may be unhappy with his situation and may not want you to get ahead in your life for fear that you will get rid of him. Don't allow this to happen!

If a friendship that you've had since you were a little girl has gone sour, either fix it or move on. Friends come and go. We all change and adapt to our world around us. But if your friends don't change with you, then you may need to start hanging out with different people. Your friends need to be people who are there for you when you need support. Women are the best listeners, and sometimes that's all we need. Girlfriends are great support when you're ready to make a new move. But they're only good if they give you the support and encouragement that you need. If your friends act resentful towards you, they may just fear the unknown. Talk to them about why you want to make your next move and what you need from them. Remember that no one is a mind reader. But if you tell them, and they're still not good to you, then you need to move on and find different people to hang out with.

You need to clean out your personal closet too. If you find that your relationships are negative and are holding you back from obtaining your goals, then you need to get rid of them just like the other clutter in your life. You need to have a clean slate. It's so difficult to make a change in your life if you have extra baggage that's holding you down. Get rid of the baggage! When your mind is not filled with worry and dismay, you will find learning new skills and thinking of new goals will be so much easier. Your mind can become cluttered with unnecessary thoughts and feelings too. Get rid of them! Get rid of the negativity, and believe in yourself! Self-esteem is a key ingredient to becoming a strong, powerful modern woman.

Make Yourself a Priority

That's what this whole book is about. I've taught you how to be aware of your environment and how you can change it. I've taught you how to play the boys' game in the business world and how to win the game playing by their rules. I've taught you how to succeed in your career. But if you don't make these changes to prioritize your life, it will never happen.

This doesn't mean that other things in your life have to go by the wayside, but you must realize that you can't be last on the list anymore if you want to make your career a success. It's ok to dedicate yourself to your family and your children, but living your life for them will only leave you to feel empty inside when it's time for them to leave—and they will always leave. This is your life, not theirs. Show your children what it means to be a powerful modern woman. If you have daughters, it's important that you teach them how to survive in the man's world when they are young. In that way when it's time for them to live life on their own, they won't be lost. They will have the survival skills needed to manage their own lives and to become successful, because you taught them what to do.

It's not a difficult thing to do, but it does require some action. Keep your notebook with your goals included. Then meet each goal with your chin held high and a big smile on your face. In that way no one will suspect that something's wrong if there's an obstacle that's in your way. If you're unhappy with your current situation, then do something about it. It doesn't have to be earth-shattering! Change can happen subtly over time. But as time progresses and you look back on the last year or two, you won't even recognize the past. Your world will have changed so much that you will realize that your world is so much better and your attitude will be too!

Get the drama out of your life once and for all! If this includes a relationship or friendship, then get rid of it. If you are to make a positive change in your life, it is critical that you have only positive thoughts in your head. Don't let others that are negative influence you or your decision to make a change in your life. Remember, this is your life, not theirs. If they want to stay in the same place as they've been for the past decade, then that's their prerogative. Don't allow anyone to rain on your parade! You've come this far; don't stop now! You can do it! I know you can! And when you look back on all that you've accomplished, you will be so proud of yourself. Then when it is time, you'll help someone else do the same thing. That's how evolution and progression take place. One step at a time and one person at a time. Start a revolution! It only takes one drop of water to start a flood. I want this book to start the flood. I want you to keep it going.

Legacy

As you go through your journey to self-improvement and self-discovery, you need to know why you're doing this! A main reason that most people want to make changes is to leave a legacy. Just think about it—this could be your legacy! The next change that you make could be the one that makes your family happy and healthy. The next problem that you will solve could make an important impact not only to you but to your community as well. Wouldn't you feel great about yourself if that becomes reality—That a little effort on your part could change others lives for the better?

Even if your strides are small, you're still doing something positive towards women everywhere. And that's all that matters. It's the strides you make everyday that accumulate over time and create a huge change in your environment. It's an empowering feeling when you become successful fulfilling your goals and making important changes and improvements in your workplace.

That's why I taught you how to pick and choose the goals you want to achieve. And at the beginning, you'll want to choose the goals that are small and that are easily achievable. This will not only reinforce the goal process, but it will also give you the confidence that you need to move onto the bigger and harder goals. It's all about the baby steps.

As you reach your goals in the workplace, you'll find that your "planning method" of doing things will spill out into your personal life too. Your family and friends will see a change in you. They won't necessarily know what that change is at first, but as you do more and more things in your life, they will see the confidence just oozing out of your pores. This confidence is usually contagious.

Your family will notice that you're much happier and that you walk with a purpose. That you have your head held high and that you're always ready to take on whatever obstacles are in your way. And your children will start to imitate this. They will start to succeed in school and in the activities that they choose to do. Their attitudes will become positive and confident.

This is the legacy that you're meant to leave to your environment. This is the legacy that you deserve to be remembered for. The strength and control of the powerful modern woman is a wonderful thing! It makes others wake up and notice that they are in the presence of something bigger than themselves: something that is very important, something that is very special, something that they must learn about, something that they are attracted to but can't explain.

As I've said before, success is contagious. Some women don't know how to achieve it, and your legacy can show others how you accomplished your main objectives in life. It's an awesome inspiring thing when you become a success, and then share your experiences with someone else. It's a privilege to be a mentor. It's the payback for all of the effort that you've just put into the projects at work. To see other women's faces light up when they achieve their objectives. To see your daughter get her first "A" on a project that you helped her with. Leaving a legacy is one of the best purposes to life. It gives you energy. It gives you pride. And it gives you the ability to see the big picture, because you've already been there and can see the end result.

So take your baby steps. Set your goals. And remember that others are watching you and they're waiting for you to become the success that they already believe that you are.

In the next chapter, I want to introduce you to a bunch of successful, interesting women that will hopefully inspire you to make changes in your life. Each of these women has struggled with their femininity in the man's world and has triumphed over adversity. I want you to read their stories and see how the changes they've made to help improve their lives can affect the way you live yours.

Chapter 6
Living In the Man's World

There are so many inspirational people in the world today that I could only include a few people that have come across my life thus far. I hope you take their stories and can learn something from them that you can use in either your personal or your professional life. Sometimes if you hear about another woman that has had the same experiences as you, you can feel a connection with that person and can soak up her advice.

That's what life is all about. It's the connections that you make and the people that you meet. When you are reading these amazing women's stories, I want you to keep an open mind and to accept them with open arms. These women tell very personal stories that can help you to achieve the success that you are looking for in your life. All of the last names of the women in the stories have been withheld for their preferred privacy but these are true stories from real women. Enjoy!

Peggy

The first story we are going to explore comes from a woman by the name of Peggy M. Peggy grew up in the 1970's in Chicago, Illinois. Peggy was one of thirteen children and was the oldest girl. She got a job at a pizza place when she was thirteen years old and paid for her own Catholic High School tuition with the money that she earned from working.

She worked and was a gifted athlete. She led her high school volleyball team to a national ranking and many awards. Due to the passing of Title IX which forced colleges to award female athletes with scholarships as well as male athletes, she received a full scholarship to Pepperdine University in California. She led her volleyball team to a third place ranking in the NCAA.

She graduated and became an assistant volleyball coach at the University of California, Santa Barbara where she was introduced to Mr. Paul Orf, founder of Kinko's. She asked him if he was hiring people, and he told her to stop by for an interview. When she got there, she was asked what she could do. Could she type? She tried and wasn't very good but said that she would learn if that was required of her. She told him that she was good with people from having a strong past experience with coaching and helping to raise a large family. He told her to go to the shipping department to see what they could do for her.

She was hired as a Special Projects Manager where she received hands-on training. She learned how to capture a vision, used her resources around her to make others better at their jobs, develop strategies for improvement, implement them, and track their successes. From there she was moved to Seattle, Washington, and became a regional manager which overlooked twelve stores. She became one of the few women managers at that level in the company. She did this for ten years. After Kinko's went from a privately held company to a public one, she was given shares for the stores that she controlled, and she sold these and got out of the business. After having four children, she decided to get away from the business world and stayed home to raise her children. Ten years later, she started to work with her brother who started his own consulting/marketing firm. She now helps to run the personnel in the office and gives her feedback to the infrastructure of the business.

I sat down with Peggy and interviewed her about her influences and experiences working in the corporate world that was predominately male oriented.

S= me/Stephanie
P= Peggy

S—Who or what inspires you to be a powerful modern woman?

P—1. My mom. She encouraged me to be independent and responsible. She taught me to have faith and to believe in myself. Dreaming, setting goals, and happiness were always priorities for her. And the best thing she taught me was to take each day one at a time.

2. Myself—I always had self-motivation. I had my own desires to be involved and was a problem-solver. Being the oldest girl out of thirteen children, I learned to work with others at an early age. I was around boys all of my life and felt very comfortable talking to them. My volleyball experiences reinforced motivation, strength, and persistence. I learned how to step out of my comfort zone when I left Chicago to go to college in California. Working at a restaurant and playing volleyball taught me both organizational and business skills that I have carried on throughout my life. Through hard work and persistence, I learned to see my goals, to believe in myself that I could do it, and then have the courage to achieve it.

S—How important is time management, organization, and communication in both your family life and your business ventures?

P—The only way things get done is through organization. You always have to start with the end result in mind, and work your way towards that result. Through organization, you can see what the crucial areas are and set your priorities. You need to use all of the skills that you posses to communicate both in your personal and professional environments.

S—How often do you set business goals? Do you immediately set new goals? How do you meet these goals?

P—Both family and business goals need to be constantly reinforced and updated. You need to start with the end in mind when you are building your goal list. You need to write down your goals and keep them in front of you at all times. You must get to the crucial areas first, and then worry about the rest. If you don't set your priorities early, your path will get clouded with everyday clutter that will take up most of your time and will prevent you from moving ahead. You must take one step at a time and not get too far ahead of yourself.

S—Our listeners know about working in the real world. Have you ever had any problems with your womanly instincts at work—especially in the male-dominated business world?

P—The Kinko's environment had always been open to the thoughts of women. The partners' wives were very instrumental to the business and the success that they had.

After working for ten years in the company, I was living in Seattle at the time. We had hired a manager that we thought was very professional, charming, and good with people. He turned out to be a complete disaster, threatening women with both physical harm and sexual advances. When I learned of this, I had talked with the partners and owner of the company about this guy, and they turned the other way. After this man had nearly assaulted another female employee, he was fired. After that I never felt the same way about the company. When the company went public, I decided to spend time with my husband and children, and they bought out my shares of the company.

S—You're now in the direct marketing business; do you present information differently to men in your company compared to women? Is it different working with family?

P—We tend to do the same thing for men as we do for women. The biggest lessons I've learned when working with family is to have both mutual respect and confidentiality. We've learned to keep the issues of the office in the office and not to let the whole family in on the conversations of the business.

S—What lessons would you teach young women, including your daughters, that may be struggling with their self-doubts and lack of self-confidence?

P—I go by "Peggy's 5 P's"

   1. Patience—To take a step back and evaluate where you truly are in your life and to know that it will take time to change it.

   2. Perspective—You need to acknowledge your talents, your likes, your ideal position, the type of people that you hang out with, and what kind of money you want to make.

   3. Persistence—You need to do research, to experience things and to learn from that experience, to ask questions, to make mistakes, and to ask more questions. Each step that you take, you must give yourself

encouragement, praise, and a hug. Surround yourself with mentors, resources, and great people that you look up to and who will give you honest feedback.

4. Profit—When you have the other three in place that equals profit. When you see it, you must believe it, and then you will achieve it.

5. Prayer—You must always ask for help and strength. If you stumble and fall, you must pick yourself up and start all over again.

S—What habits would you encourage our readers to pursue? To get rid of?

P—Positive habits—Have a positive mental attitude, vision creation, goal setting, exercise, and to smile. You need to surround yourself with the type of person that you want to become. You need to use your resources and give back to others.

The irony of my success is that with all that I've achieved in my life, I sometimes feel as though I'm a failure as a parent. My first husband died of brain cancer when my two oldest children were just toddlers. After that I worked and tried to raise my children on my own. I came into contact again with an old friend from Chicago, and after he stood me up on our first date, we ended up having a long-distance relationship for two years and then got married. I had two more children with my new husband and decided after my buy-out with Kinko's that I would stay with the children at home and turn my energy and efforts towards my family. They've always had trouble in school, and I have felt almost guilty that they've been put through everything from their past.

I've recently started working with my brother and have used my talents and previous business skills to help him grow a multi-million dollar business.

I learned a lot from Peggy. I have gotten to know her over the past year and have had a few wonderful conversations with her. She has taught me that no matter how successful you've become in life, that there's always some improvement that you must have. If you believe in yourself and put some effort into your ventures, that there's no way that you can fail! I feel very honored to have met such an extraordinary woman and hope that you also can meet those that are like Peggy. They will blow your mind away! Thanks Peggy!

Kathy

The next woman I want you to meet is a woman that I've come to know on a personal level in the past two years is Kathy M. Kathy grew up in a household with an alcoholic father. He died when she was fifteen years old; her mother lost her will to live. She would yell and say discouraging things to Kathy and her siblings. After her dad died, Kathy decided to take care of her siblings and give them the life that she and they deserved. She decided that there would be no alcohol in the house and that through her actions, she would become a role model.

She studied and received her Master's in Education and got a job working as a Special Education teacher. She always considered herself as an "idea" person and wanted to either get her doctorate or do something else. She was at the bottom of her class in high school and wasn't voted to do much with her life. She knew she didn't want to be a salesperson but felt that she had so much more to give to the world around her. She was divorced with two kids and thought about going to law school. She was approached by one of her mentors to join Mary Kay Cosmetics and instead of working for someone else; she would work for herself and help others achieve their dream. She hated the idea of selling lipstick. She turned to her religious beliefs and asked God to help her learn to like Mary Kay. She was one of the first women with a Master's Degree to get into the management side of the business as a Director and recruited others that also were professional women to become part of the organization—they saw that if she could do it and become successful, they could too!

She joined Mary Kay and in nine months became a Director. For fourteen years, she did it all. She was divorced, raised two children, worked as a teacher, and did Mary Kay. Then after fourteen years, she was making enough money in the upper management of the Mary Kay organization to quit her job as a school teacher and focus her energy on building her Mary Kay business. At this point in time, she is on her way to becoming a National Sales Director which is an honor that is only achieved by two hundred out of almost two million consultants worldwide! I interviewed Kathy about her life and the way she's achieved so much with all of the obstacles around her, and here's what she said ...

S= me/Stephanie
K= Kathy

S—Who or what inspires you to be a powerful modern woman?

K—I never had a woman role model growing up. I had to look into my own heart and find out what I wanted in my life. After my dad died when I was fifteen, I knew that I didn't want to live that way, and I didn't want my family to turn out like my father did. I knew I had to make a change. I don't consider myself as a powerful modern woman at all. I consider myself a servant-based leader. I take a "heart" role. In the movie *Jerry Maguire*, one of her favorite quotes is, "If you don't have it in here (points to her heart), it doesn't matter if it's in here (points to her head.)" I wish not to be a powerful modern woman but more of a service-based leader. Helping others is the greatest power one could have. Mary Kay always had time to help others. She would make the effort to help others get what they wanted by giving them her time and knowledge of the business world.

S—How important is time management, organization, and communication in both your family life and your business ventures?

K—I did both teaching and Mary Kay for fourteen years. I became a director in nine months, full time teacher, and had a three year old at one point. You need organization and a plan for everyday. I would get up at 4:30AM; workout and listen to my religious tapes, shower and get ready, and make a hot breakfast for my children every morning. No matter what was going on in my life, I wanted my children to "wake up with excellence"—with all my love and attention. No matter how crazy the day got, I knew they at least had a warm breakfast to start their day.

Organization is very important if you're going to get things done.

I asked myself-
1. What do you want?—If your health is crap, you're done. All the money won't take care of your body. There's no excuse. Put your treadmill at the foot of your bed with your workout gear and your tennis shoes and get up in the morning and start your day off right. When your body and mind are in the right place, the day seems to go easier. It increases your endorphins.
2. Income—if you do it all sometimes you get depressed. Exercise and organization give you the strength to go on. Sometimes money isn't everything.
3. Feed your mind and your soul. Do you feel like a great woman? Like a wonderful mother? Do what it takes to feel that way.
4. Systems are important—need role model to help you. Without it you won't go far.

S—How often do you set business goals? Do you immediately set new goals? How do you meet these goals? When did you know that it was time to take your business on a regional and then national level?

K—I am constantly evolving but I feel like I am on a journey with no arrival. I have to be goal-oriented, because I feel like you never fully arrive when you own your own business. When you're in school, the endpoint is a degree. When you own your own business, you never see the end; you are always changing and trying to learn different things to improve your business. Some people need a 9-5 structure and others are more creative and want to try to make a difference in the world and do it their way. But you need vision. You can't always depend on someone else to feed your vision like a boss.

You also need a "spiritual center" or a call to purpose. I find myself to always be in discovery mode. If you show up and are willing to work, you will find success in your endeavors, but you must be willing to do the work that is necessary. You can't expect someone else to do the work for you—it doesn't work that way.

Sometimes if you want something you need to ask! A funny story comes to mind when I hear that saying. Last year, my grandson wanted the new Xbox 360. I had been having a rough year in my personal life and wasn't paying attention to the trends that were going on. Anyways, I usually am the first one in line when it comes to things like that. I remember it was a couple of days before Christmas, and I was scrambling for presents. I knew that he had wanted a new Xbox. I knew it was a long shot, but I was in the store and asked the clerk if they had any more Xboxes in the back. About ten minutes later, he had a large box in his hands—it was an Xbox that someone just had returned, and no one had picked it up yet. Everyone around me just looked at me as I put this huge box in my cart and my grandson got his Xbox that year. See, all you have to do is ask, and you never know what will happen!

You must always set new goals. You must ask yourself—"what are you going to do?" And no matter what kind of obstacles get in your way or bring you down, you must get up again and again and again. Good habits bring success. Do something towards your goal everyday. If you screw up, take responsibility, and get back up! That's the only way that progress happens.

S—What habits would you encourage our readers to pursue? To get rid of?

K—To wait for things to happen. You have to go out and do something to make it happen. If you want to be successful in life, you must find that inner strength that I believe everyone has and then use it to make things happen. Then if things get hard, keep going. As long as you don't stop, you'll always progress forward.

I always feel inspired when I talk with Kathy. She's always a very encouraging person and finds the strengths in everyone which is a special gift that not everyone has. Kathy's life has been a roller coaster ride but through it all, she's kept her faith not only in God but also in herself that no matter what, she'll be alright. That's an awesome feeling to have!

Becky

The next woman on the roster is Becky K. Becky grew up not knowing what she wanted to do with her life. She entered Baldwin Wallace College and signed up for a bunch of science classes. She had an interest in medicine but didn't want the large loans and a lifetime of long hours. So she decided to major in biology and look for a job. Her dad, a high school biology teacher, told her that there weren't many jobs in the field other than teaching or lab tech work and that she should have a "Plan B" in case biology didn't work out. He told her that "she would end up shoveling poo at the zoo" if she didn't have something to fall back on.

She only needed a few more classes for a chemistry major, so she decided to pick that up. In her senior year she attended a lecture. The main speaker was the head of a cancer research program. She was fascinated with this and decided to pursue it. She then entered Kent State University's Master's program.

After she finished her Master's degree, she realized in her industrial career that she needed a Ph.D. to implement her own research ideas instead of taking others' direction. So she went back to Kent State and got her PhD in materials chemistry. She then managed to get a couple of different positions in polymer chemistry. This past year, she decided that she was more interested in the business side of technology and resigned her R&D position in the lab.

I sat down with Becky and inquired about the following.

S= me/Stephanie
B= Becky

S—Who or what inspires you to be a powerful modern woman?

B—My mother. My mother is a great example of a powerful modern woman. She runs and directs thirteen small companies. She always worked more hours than my dad who was a teacher and always had the summer and holidays off. But she was always there doing the "typical" motherly things, making sure we were taken care of.

My grandmother was also an inspiration. She was a full-time nurse and had six kids. She worked *and* still managed to take care of everyone. She's 82 now and still runs around in heels and cuts her own grass. She thinks that "age is just a number." She said that she saw an interview with Sophia Loren and they asked her how she stays looking so young. She replied that she always takes the stairs—no matter how tired she feels. So my grandmother takes the stairs.

S—Our listeners know about working in the real world, have you ever had any problems with your womanly instincts at work?

B—YES, YES, YES! It's hard being a woman and working in a male-dominated field like chemistry. Sometimes I'd be in a conference room with fifteen people, and I'd be the only woman there. It's also difficult because my field is international, and not many cultures see woman as equal partners. My former company worked with a Japanese company who had women engineers. These women had the same degrees as their male counterparts, but they were the ones serving the coffee and donuts and cleaning up afterwards. Sometimes it's difficult to assimilate to their way, but you need to be tactful when asserting yourself but in a non-aggressive style.

S—Do you present information differently to men in your company compared to women?

B—Yes. Women can have different styles of communication in the workplace. Some are very direct, and some come off as "flirty." When communicating with the opposite sex, women need to play down any gender differences that there may be so that they will earn the respect of their male counterparts. Men are very visual creatures. Women must be very conscious of their postures and the way they are dressed. If they draw attention to the wrong body parts, they will lose the respect of the male crowd and their credibility will be shot.

If a woman does find herself in a compromising situation, she needs to draw the line and make sure that the other people know where she stands. Be comfortable in yourself, but don't draw the wrong kind of attention at the same time.

S-Do you struggle with communication problems in other areas of your life?

B—I've always struggled with communicating with others because I tend to be very direct and honest with my answers. I am totally opposite to my husband Doug, which seems to work out well in our marriage. He's the thinker. He'll stop, reflect, think and analyze an issue before he responds. I tend to jump right in which can sometimes be a problem. But I feel that women who are quiet, timid and soft-spoken rarely make history. The greatest rewards usually have the greatest risks.

S—How do you find the time to juggle your career and your family? I know that you're pregnant with your second child?

B—You just do what you have to do. I do the full-time mom stuff, and then I work out of the house. You need a cooperative husband if you're going to get everything done that needs to get done. Weekends are difficult because all we do is run around and do errands, but you must do what you can.

S—You've accomplished so much in your life already, what goals do you have for your future?

B—Since I'm in between jobs right now, I'm open to anything. I'd like something more fast-paced and business oriented.

S—Is goal-setting an important attribute that you possess?

B—I think that goal-setting is very important if you're going to do what you want to do. There's a difference between a dream and a goal. A dream is a fantasy that has no plan. Most women that dream aren't fulfilled. A goal is a plan that you actively take steps to achieve. All successful women have goals. So I have to say that you should definitely be a goal-oriented woman and not a dreamer.

S—What lessons would you teach young women out there that may be struggling with their self-doubts and lack of self-confidence?

B-As far as those girls that have self-doubt—you need to get rid of it. If you don't believe in yourself, no one will. You need to keep your head held high when you walk in a room, and then people will know that you command respect. Be confident but not arrogant! You need to know the difference between being assertive and being aggressive. Be passionate but not "emotional." Be professional but likeable.

S—What habits would you encourage our readers to pursue? To get rid of?

B—This goes with the previous question. You must be passionate about your career but not termed "emotional" by your male crowd. I learned the hard way my first year in the workforce that ninety percent of what you say is *how* you say it and not *what* you say! Be tactful but assertive.

The last thing I want to say is that it's sometimes difficult to work with others. Sometimes other people fall short of your expectations. This is normal; if everyone was as smart or as talented as you are, they'd be doing your job without you! Be patient but firm, and you should be successful.

I noticed that as I was talking with Becky that she had the same philosophies as I do about women and men in the business world. I guess all powerful modern women do have the same way of thinking! I hope that you start thinking like this too—if you do, you're sure to be a success no matter what you want to do in your life

Sharon

The next woman I want you to read about is Sharon S. Sharon grew up in Detroit, Michigan and pursued a career in education. She received a scholarship to Michigan State University but decided to go to Wayne State, because they had a strong education curriculum. She received a Bachelor's degree in education and a Master's in psychology. She then taught in Detroit for seven years doing elementary education in their inner-city school district. In her last year, she became the curriculum director for the school in which she was teaching.

Her husband had just received his PhD in speech pathology and was offered a position in Ohio at the University of Akron. He accepted the position, and then she was forced to find another job. Since she worked with directing curriculum in Detroit, she was able through people that she knew to find a position with the Kent State University in the early-childhood department as well as helping with student teachers at the University of Akron.

She was at a women's networking event and met a woman who was a real estate agent. After talking with her, she decided to pursue real estate. She got her license and was an independent agent in 1984 and then decided to start her own agency. She had a partner who was in insurance and after five years, he suddenly died. She found herself in a pickle and decided that she couldn't run her agency on her own and closed it. She took a job a Coldwell Banker Realty in 1990 which was bought out by Hunter Realty a year after.

She noticed that with Coldwell Banker, it was very corporate. She had a lot of managers to go through when she wanted an idea implemented, and she became very frustrated with that. But when Hunter Realty bought them, she only had to answer to the president of the company. She found that things went through very easily and quickly. The president of the company is very creative and encourages his employees to be that way too and to express their thoughts and opinions on issues that come up.

I sat down with Sharon on the phone for an interview and here's the rest of it....

S= me/Stephanie
SS= Sharon

S—Who or what inspires you to be a powerful modern woman?

SS—My mother. She always encouraged me to be self-reliant and to have a vision. I'm the only child and she always encouraged me to keep the course.

S—How did you first get into real estate?

SS—I met a lady in a women's club when I first moved to Ohio. She also was from Detroit, and we hit it off. She and my husband encouraged me to get into real estate. They both thought I would do a good job.

S—Now that you're in an executive position in the company, how important are communication skills between you and your employees?

SS—They're very important, especially between me and the employees as well as the independent real estate agents that we deal with. Communication between me and the employees are really important because they have to deal with the independent agents, and sometimes they abuse the employees. So I play the diplomat when problems arise. My psychology degree as well as my education background has helped me tremendously with my position at Hunter.

S—Do you find that there's a difference in the way that you approach women versus male agents?

SS—No. I don't approach them any differently. Before when I was selling real estate, both women and men equally made the buying decisions. Now we find that the largest growth in the buying market is single women—forty-eight percent. I used to match women agents with women buyers and so forth, but I had a couple of times that that strategy backfired. Now I try to match up the personality types and not sex or racial background.

S—How do you help those women that want to change their careers and get into the real estate field?

SS—I get a lot of leads from people that are interested in getting in the field. A lot of men are getting back into it. I encourage them *not* to give up their job until their new career is up and running and it's on track. It's like buying a house—you want to sell your house first; and then buy another one, or else you might have two mortgages at the same time. This creates a lot of stress.

I tell them that they need to do the classes at their own speed, and take the test. Then they need Coldwell Banker University training to fill in the gaps that the classes don't cover. We teach them how to get business, how to network, deal with title work, and enforce communication skills. This helps with referrals and comradery. They also work with a mentor for three months to help them with business plans and time management which is important with the women that are doing two careers.

They usually want to change careers because of the flexibility that real estate offers. It's not a nine to five job. You have your own company and this is the smallest investment into a company that you can have. If you were to buy a franchise, it may cost you hundreds of thousands of dollars just to start the business. With real estate, it only costs a couple hundred dollars to go through the classes and join the state board and multiple listing services. The sky is the limit.

If they don't have all of the money, they can just do the classes and pass the test, and they can join Person-to-Person Realty which is a subsidiary of Coldwell Banker. They don't have to belong to the board of realtors. They can be real estate agents, but they can't write up any contracts. They can work with an agent and get the referral fees. They can do open houses and show houses but still work with another agent. This allows them to get experience and on-the-job training. They can save for their board and MLS fees.

S—How important is organization in your life?

SS—It's essential to getting anything done. It affects both my personal and my professional life. The more organized I am, the more productive I am. I always write a goal list so that I know what I'm doing the next day. We teach time management and organizational skills in the Coldwell Banker University.

S—Is your husband very supportive?

SS—Absolutely! He does all of the cooking which frees up a lot of time for me.

S—If our readers are interested in real estate, what characteristics must they possess?

SS—The first one is the most important one, and that is tenacity. You don't have to bug people, but you do have to follow-up with people, and keep things on course. When I came to this office, the top producer was named Carol. She was very tenacious and kept that up until she died. She would always keep going back to people, in a nice way, until she got results.

One needs to communicate and be a good listener. You must also have enthusiasm. Keep in touch with your buyers just to let them know what is going on. Always keep them reassured. Hold their hands and give them the confidence in you that you will take care of them.

One thing that people can do is to walk in the shoes of an agent in a simulator. They can go to www.cbhunter.com. Click on "Career in Real Estate" then take the real estate simulator test. It takes about an hour to go through the different scenarios that they have on the website. After they do that, they send me their results, and then I contact the prospect and go over the results with them. We then talk about the skills that they posses and we tell them if we think that they would be a good match for the real estate business.

S—What habits do you encourage our readers to pursue? To get rid of?

SS—Take the time to get organized and maintain it. Try not to procrastinate. Carol got to the point where she wouldn't do something if it wasn't done right away. She was afraid to lose business.

It was very interesting talking to Sharon. She's been in the business for many years and has shown me that your talents and skills that you learn in school can be used in various ways. She went from an educational background with children to an educational opportunity with real estate. She also taught me the importance of networking. If she hadn't done some networking when she first moved to Ohio, she may have missed an opportunity to become a success in the real estate field.

Sometimes you just have to take a leap of faith. If you believe in yourself and allow others to believe in you too, you're sure to have success. Look at Sharon, with her mom's encouragement; she's become a success by just following her gut instincts.

Gretchen

The next woman I want to introduce you to is Gretchen B. Gretchen grew up in a small town in Ohio and was one of seven children. Being the oldest child, Gretchen was taught at an early age the importance of independence and to help do what it took to get the job done.

She went to Catholic school and then to John Carroll University, a private college in Ohio where she met her husband John. They both graduated and got married and then she followed him to dental school, and later to his oral surgery residency in Chicago, IL. She had to help support them and got a job at a company that sold commercial office furniture, doing customer service. She then became pregnant within the first month that she was in Chicago with their first child. Her company was very flexible, and she continued to work during her first pregnancy. She worked full-time after her daughter was born and got a few promotions. She got pregnant again with her second child. Gretchen started to work at home part-time—two days a week and three days at the office to help offset daycare which was, and still is, very expensive. She found out that she could accomplish more from home than she did at the office. After John's residency program was over, they decided to move back to Ohio to be closer to their families. She became pregnant with her third child and later had her fourth.

I sat down with Gretchen for an interview and here's what she had to say …

S= me/Stephanie
G= Gretchen

S-Who or what inspires you to be a powerful modern woman?

G—My mom was very strong-willed and independent. She was a "take-charge" kind of lady. She was the first one to inspire me to think on my own and not to rely on anyone else to take care of me. She encouraged me to go back to work after all of my pregnancies.

I also seem to be influenced by the people around me. My husband John, I met in college and he was and still is very goal-oriented and was the Type-A personality. This helped to push me to my limits. I encourage all of you to surround yourself with people that will raise you up and take you to the next level. I think that's very important.

S—You have four children under the age of 11, how do you balance your life between working and raising your family?

G—The big thing is that you need to know your limits. My house isn't perfect. I can't be the CEO. I only have so much time during the day. I don't try to do everything or be everything to everyone. I don't volunteer for everything. I try my best, and that's all that I can do. I don't have a lot of extra time—I don't watch TV. When you grow up one of seven kids, you're used to chaos around you—all that you can do is to take a deep breath, and jump into the action.

You need to prioritize and don't over-extend yourself. You need to learn how to say "NO." It's ok to not do everything. Most women try to please everyone and only make themselves miserable, I've learned not to do that.

S—What roles do you and your husband share?

G—When he was doing his residency, it was ninety percent me and maybe ten percent him. But now he helps out equally. He takes a couple of the kids in the morning, and I only have a couple of them to deal with and get ready for school. He takes the kids to practice and drops them off. I'll stay at home and clean up the house and get meals ready to go. It definitely takes two people to raise four kids. He's more the disciplinarian than I am, and I think that things are getting easier since they're getting older, and they're not little babies anymore.

S—How much influence does organization and goal-setting have in your everyday life?

G—It has a lot to do with it. Organization is not something that comes naturally to me—it's something I work on all of the time. But I find that more things get done when I stay on track with my organizational skills. I'm also a procrastinator, and I try to get out of that cycle. I have a hard work-ethic and am high energy. This helps to offset any chaos or unorganized areas that I may find myself into.

One thing that I've learned over the years is that I can't be organized for everyone. If my child forgets to tell me that he's out of lunch tickets, I don't go out of my way to go to the school and get him one. This not only disrupts my day, but it teaches my child that I will not bail him out of trouble every time he forgets something. This doesn't teach them anything. They've learned that it's their responsibility to keep track of their own things, and I think that this is a very valuable lesson that you need to teach your children.

As far as goals are concerned—if I want something, I set a goal and work for it. I just ran the city marathon in under four hours this year, and that was a goal that I had had for some time; I finally did it. I did a lot of training for it and had to make the time to do it everyday even when it got hard.

S—What do you want to share with my readers about "having it all"—being a powerful modern woman *and* a wife and mother?

G—If you want to "have it all" you have to learn that you can't control every aspect in your life. You have to learn to let it go; let things happen and fall into place. When you're a mom and a working woman, your life is not about "fun;" it's about helping to mold your children and getting things done that need to get done. Sometimes things drive me crazy, but I never pretend that I have everything in control. I just let things happen and try not to be a control freak.

S—You have two daughters, what are you going to teach them about how to be a powerful modern woman? Will you encourage them to have the same kind of life that you have? A career, family, and social life?

G—I am always hard on myself. Most moms want more for their kids than what they've had or done. I never knew what I wanted to do with my life when I was young. I encourage my girls to set their life goals early and to not let things get in the way of those goals. My oldest daughter wants to travel and go away to school which John and I encourage her to do.

I also discourage her to be "boy crazy." I didn't dream of my wedding day when I was a young girl or want a certain number of kids, and I don't encourage her to be that way either. I think with two annoying little brothers, her craziness for boys won't get out of hand.

I think that all kids have choices and that my mom always reinforced my decisions in life. She always encouraged me to work and to be independent.

S—What habits would you encourage our readers to pursue? To get rid of?

G—I definitely encourage people to be independent. You need to rely on yourself and make your own decisions. Once you are married and have children, it's easy to lose your independence, because you're doing things for other people.

Realize that you're not perfect and that you can't do everything perfectly. Sometimes you feel as if you're constantly apologizing to everyone, but get rid of the guilt and learn how to say "NO." For those working moms out there, you must realize that if you want to be seen as an equal in the workforce, you need to put in equal work. If your child is sick, if you need to take time off from work to take care of your child, then you must make up the work that you've missed. If you need to take it home with you, then do it. If you don't, you may be criticized by others for your lack of a contribution to the project. Don't dump your problems on others and never miss deadlines!

I was very inspired my talking to Gretchen. Here's a lady that is financially independent from her husband who himself makes good money. But through a family and the ups and downs of marriage, she's still kept her independence. I admire that. Sometimes we all take the easy way out. We meet Mr. Wonderful that makes good cash, and we decide that we can give up our career and stay at home with the family. But what we don't know is that we also give up our freedom and our independence. If you get a divorce down the road, you will have a tough time finding the financial means necessary to take care of your family and have the lifestyle that you're used to. You can't make up for the time that you've lost for all of those promotions that you passed up. You never get that back.

Gretchen helped to reinforce the idea that if you work hard at something, you will succeed in doing it. But you have to work at it. If you want to work and have a family, you can't be the Stepford Wife. Things won't be perfect, and if someone thinks that she should, then she needs to have her head examined, because it's just not a realistic thing.

Stacey

The next woman I want to introduce to you is one of my best friends who is partly responsible for helping me become the powerful modern woman that I am today. You could say that Stacey K. was my first mentor.

Stacey K. grew up in a small town in Ohio. She was the only girl in the family and had an older brother. Her dad owned a service station, and her mom stayed home and helped her dad by doing the station books. Stacey was an athlete in school, was in the "popular group," and then went on to Mount Union College where she received a degree in Biology. After she graduated from college, she worked for GE for two years and applied to multiple pharmaceutical companies. She got an entry level sales representative job, and got promoted over the next nine years to a senior sales representative and to an executive sales representative position.

I sat down with Stacey for an interview and here's what she had to say ...

S= me/Stephanie
ST= Stacey

S-Who or what inspires you to be a powerful modern woman?

ST—I think the simple fact that I am the first member of my family to graduate from college has inspired me to continue to be a powerful modern woman. The little bit of doubt my family and friends had about me finishing college pushed me to be independent. I started to look at my future as mine, and I was determined not to fall into the pattern of life the other females in my family had—they got married, stayed at home with the kids, and took care of their husbands. I wanted to stand on my own two feet and not depend on someone else to take care of me.

S—How important is time management and organization not only in your personal life but in your business ventures?

ST—Time management and organization are the key ingredients to my everyday life. I use a planner daily to keep my appointments straight and to plan out my personal time. Since I am single, not only am I the sole-bread winner, but I am also the cleaning lady and the landscaper. So as you can see, I need to plan out all of my daily events to not only fit in my demanding job but my other responsibilities as a home owner, friend, and family member.

As for my work day, I plan my month in advance day by day. This allows me to keep on task and make sure all deadlines are met. Each night I sit down to assess what tasks I have completed that day and what might still need to be done; then plan accordingly for the next day. So YES, organization and time management are key to success.

S—You're a big list person, how important is making a daily list of your goals?

ST—It's very important to get your goals done each and everyday. I break my business goals up into daily, weekly, monthly, and yearly goals. I feel that you can't say, "This is what I want to accomplish," at the beginning of the year and not look at your goal list until the end of the year. You need to be continuously assessing your goals and how or if you are hitting those goals. You may find that after the first quarter, your goals are set too low or are clearly not obtainable based on the market trends. By looking at my goals often, I have developed into a very successful pharmaceutical representative over the years.

The other aspect of goal-setting is to know who can help you obtain your goals. For example, I will generally think of twenty specific customers and hyper-focus on them during a three to six month period. I will make sure I have more face-to-face time with these customers including appointments over breakfast, lunch, and dinner or during cold calls when I know they are available. It's amazing how powerful attention to detail is. It can definitely earn you more time and business if done correctly.

S-Your business is made up of both men and women, what is the difference in your communication styles between men and women?

ST—Many times I try to look at my customers based on personality rather than sex. You will find that many people want to just get to the point and want the "bottom line" information. Others will want to be your friend and have a lot of social talk in between business. Others will be extremely analytical and just want the facts. So I tend to try to pinpoint their personality first and foremost.

However, the sex of the customer does come into play when it comes to relationship-building. Men want to be seen as the strong, smart leaders. I have found that when I am communicating with male customers, I need to meet their need of feeling this way before I will earn their trust and their respect. I have to "recognize" their dominance and not try to be the "alpha dog." Women on the other hand, don't want to feel "threatened."

S—Being an executive sales representative and a mentor to many people, what habits would you encourage others to pursue? To get rid of?

ST—The best advice I can give is to be organized not only in your professional life but also in your personal life. You will find more projects finished sooner than later which leads to other projects being started sooner. Before you know it, you are ahead of schedule for the year, and you'll hit your goals ahead of schedule too.

Another factor to my success is standing up for myself. Don't let anyone tell you that you can't do something. You don't know until you try. If you try and fail, try again but in a different way. If scientists gave up every time they failed, we wouldn't have computers or drugs that we have today. Get rid of the "defeatist" trait.

Stacey and I hung out and studied together in college. She taught me what it took to take my dreams and goals to the next level. That's what a mentor does. She helped me, and I helped her at the same time. I can't stress enough the "support" factor. When you are trying to achieve your goal(s) it is of utmost importance to have someone in your corner motivating you and listening to you when you need to vent.

She was and still is one of my personal inspirations in life. She accomplishes what she sets her mind to, and I admire that and strive to be that way in my own life. Thanks for always being there for me!

Amanda

The next woman that I want to introduce you to is Amanda F. Amanda grew up in Ohio and then attended Mount Union College and received a Bachelor's degree in Communications and German. She got married to her college sweetheart shortly after college. She started working for a small manufacturing company and earned as many promotions as the company had to offer.

After five years, she started to have trouble in her marriage. She had her first child and decided that she had gone as far with her job as she could. She decided that she would get into the insurance/financial planning business. She was lucky that her dad had been part of that business for over thirty years and could steer her in the right direction. She eventually got divorced and realized that she not only had herself to support, but also a daughter. She joined her dad's company and started to go back to school to learn the ins and outs of the financial services and insurance business. She is currently finishing up her CFP (certified financial planner) designation and her CLU (insurance underwriting).

I sat down with Amanda for an interview and here's what she had to say ...

S= me/Stephanie
A= Amanda

S—Who or what inspires you to be a powerful modern woman?

A—I feel inspiration out of necessity. I think it's a choice and what determines that choice is what is most important to you. In my case, it's my daughter. I am inspired to be independent as an example for her. I want her growing up knowing that she is capable.

S—The insurance business is dominantly men. Have you had any difficulty breaking through the barriers that the men's world have put in front of you? How do you deal with men—is there a difference in your approach with them? Do you have problems communicating with them?

A—I find more barriers with my age than with my gender. I don't fit the financial advisor stereotype of a middle-aged man with a comb-over. Normally that's an initial reaction though, and once I start building a relationship with a client, it's not an issue.

Occasionally, I will meet with a client or prospect that has a problem dealing with women. In fact, my first week on the job I went to a potential client's house and the husband refused to meet with me. He sat in an adjoining room barking out commands to his wife. I wasn't sure what to do at the time. If that happened to me today though, I would politely invite him to join us or would simply move on and not waste anymore time.

How I deal with men depends on how they are. Some of my best clients are wonderful men. If I find one that's difficult, I simply won't pursue business with him or send him to another advisor. That's one beauty of being self-employed.

As far as communication, again I think it depends on the person. If he is analytical, I will be analytical and explain all the details. If I'm dealing with a driver then I just cut right to the chase, give him the summary, etc. This is where my background in communications has really served me—being able to adapt how I communicate based on the person I'm dealing with.

Then there are the men that will talk to you just because you are female. Those are sometimes fun because it's interesting to see how they change their tone, mannerisms, etc. once they realize that you have it together and know what you're talking about!

S—You started your business out of necessity. You were going through a divorce and had a child to raise. What importance have you placed on your goal-setting skills and the ability that you possess to carry them out?

A—It's very important to me to have a vision and then declare it. In my mind goals are just the stepping stones to whatever your vision is. Because my daughter is important to me and because I want to show her how to be capable, I have been able to refine these skills. For me, I first decide what my vision is. Then I declare it. By saying it out loud and by telling those who are important to me, it becomes real. At that point I feel obligated to complete the vision … because it's my word. Then the goal setting becomes easy. I've determined what I want. I know it. Everyone knows it, and the goals are simply the steps to get there.

S—You've accomplished so much in your life already, what goals do you have for your future?

A—Personal goals relate primarily to my daughter and things I want to teach her. For example, the importance of giving to others. Every year now for her birthday, she picks out what she wants to donate. Last year it was shoes. What five-year old knows what charity is?

Business wise, I want to finish my professional designations and then bring in a newer associate to work with some of our clients that don't require as much planning. I would also like to expand the courses that I teach at the college level and have already made some progress with other community colleges.

S—What lessons would you teach young women out there that may be struggling with their self-doubts and lack of self-confidence?

A—Get over it. You're wasting your own time. Learn to be happy by choosing to be so. Don't apologize for knowing what you want. If you don't know what you want, think it through. Don't ever base your personal happiness on the opinions of others.

S—What habits would you encourage our readers to pursue? To get rid of?

A—I think it's important to get your education, even if you have every intention of getting married and being a stay-at-home mom. No one can take your education from you, and it gives you an exit strategy in case the fairy tale doesn't happen.

A habit to keep? Always have a vision, something to strive for.
A habit to ditch? Making excuses.

I went to college with Amanda, but I wasn't very close to her as I was with some of my other friends. But after her divorce, she moved in my neighborhood, and I've gotten to know her better. I feel that Amanda and I have a lot of similarities. We both built our businesses from scratch out of necessity. We both went through tough divorces that shook us to our cores and made us think about what kind of women we wanted to be. But like the saying goes—you're only given what you can handle. And I think Amanda's handled her problems with grace and dignity. She pulled herself up off the ground, brushed herself off, and told the world that she was ready for another fight. Thanks Amanda!

Della

The last woman that I want you to meet is Della C. Della grew up in Ohio as the only child of a rubber factory worker. Her dad was twenty years older than her mom and when Della was a little girl; her dad had retired from the rubber plant. Della remembers many fond memories of the time she spent with her dad. When she had to go to different school functions, her dad would take her and then go spend time with his friends playing cards.

Della grew up wanting to be a dentist. She applied to the University of Kentucky and was accepted to their Pre-Dental program. She went to Europe that summer and her Dad forgot to send the money for school and they cancelled all of her classes and she found herself without a plan. It was too late to get into school after she returned from Europe and decided to go to a trade school. After working for six months as a dental assistant, she enrolled at Kent State University switching her major to secondary education with a French major and English minor. In her third year she met Doug, got married, and quit school.

Soon after that she found herself pregnant with her daughter. After her daughter was born, her marriage went down the tubes and she got divorced. She knew that school was out and she decided to get a job at the front desk in a dental office where she's been ever since.

I sat down with Della for an interview and here's what she had to say …

S= me/Stephanie
D= Della

S—Who or what inspires you to be a powerful modern woman?

D—My mom, Sophia. She was the most influential person in my life. She came from a lot of adversity in her life and rose above it. For example, my grandfather was a Greek engineer who moved to Alexandria to help build the canals and sewer systems in the early 1900's. He was bitten by some kind of bug, and the infection spread until it finally killed him. My mom was nine and my uncle was only four years old when my grandpa died. My grandma soon died of an aneurysm while she was hanging up clothes. My Great-Aunt came to live with them to help raise them. They had no money coming in and had to live on a government stipend (like social security.) My mom got straight A's, so she could get a scholarship and go to school for free. My mom and uncle only got one uniform for the entire school year and had to wash it every night for the next day.

My mom went on to college and then worked at a newspaper in the distribution area and helped support her family and brother. My uncle came to the U.S. to finish his college degree. He graduated from Kent State University and got a job. My mom moved to the U.S. too, and later met my dad and got married.

S—Dealing with the public/customer service is not an easy job. What communication skills have you acquired over the years to help deal with the obstacles involved with speaking to the public?

D—The biggest problem in dealing with people that are in pain or are clueless about their problems is that they are frightened and are dealing with the unknown. You need to listen and be sympathetic to their pain, and if you do, they'll react to you in a kind way. They'll realize that you're trying to help them, and you're not blowing them off. It may not be a true emergency but to them it is. Don't make them feel as if they're just another face in your office. They need to know that someone's there to listen to them and to take care of them no matter what happens.

S—How important is organization to your life?

D—You have to organize things by priority. Do the most important things first, and then the rest will follow.

S—You were divorced from your first husband when your daughter was only a toddler. How did you raise your child AND work? What struggles did you go through? What lessons did you learn from that experience?

D—Don't have a kid unless you can afford it. Don't expect anyone to help you because having a child is your responsibility. You're going to make sacrifices—you're going to miss a lot of stuff when you're single, and you have to work. But the bottom line is that the job can't suffer, because you need to make money to put food on the table. It's a pride-thing not to take a hand-out which I never did.

S—Have you ever had any problems with your communication skills at work?

D—Not really. I put everyone on the same table, and it seems to work. Sometimes I have a lighter touch with women.

S—What lessons would you teach young women out there that may be struggling with their self-doubts and lack of self-confidence?

D—If you know your stuff, then you won't have an issue with people.

S—What habits would you encourage others to pursue? To get rid of?

D—The best habit to have is a good work ethic. Your co-workers depend on you, and if you're not there, they will have to pull the weight for you; this will build up resentment. Also be helpful; if you offer to help someone, you're bound to have it come back to you.

I discourage gossip at work. This only can bring problems in the office. Keep your comments to yourself and work together as a team. It'll make things go faster and smoother.

It seems like Della's family history unquestionably shaped her life. It goes to show you that you may have bad cards dealt to you but that you can overcome those cards by playing the game to the best of your abilities. You can never give up even though you may have to take a different course than what you first anticipated.

Conclusion

I hope you've learned how to use your femininity to your advantage. I wish you the best in all of your endeavors. It only takes a spark to start a fire. But you have to believe in yourself enough to either start or continue your life's journey. And don't worry; we all make stupid mistakes. But the winners are the ones that jump back up and throw themselves into the battle.

The women that I've met and written about in this book all have one thing in common—they're all women who have hearts of gold! They know that they can make a difference in this world, and they take each day one by one. They have the spirit of the powerful modern day woman! And I know that you have that same fighting spirit inside you. You may not believe me, but I know it's true. All women are natural born fighters. We've come so far in civilization. Don't let anyone or anything keep you down. If you're lost and need a mentor, don't be afraid to ask someone that you admire for some help.

If you're one of the powerful modern women, don't be afraid to give back to your community. You may be able to help countless women change their lives into something that they and their families can be proud of. You never know, you may help them reach their "Perfect Day." Do me a favor; give this book to a friend. Give this book to someone you know that may be down and out. Give this book to your teenager or college daughter that may need a little encouragement as she fights her own struggles. Just pass it on—you may change someone's life forever.

About the Author

Dr. Stephanie Aldrich is a general dentist and owner of Akron Dental Concepts, LLC one of the largest female-owned dental practices in the city of Akron, Ohio. In 2006, she was awarded the Fellowship of the Academy of General Dentistry, an honor only 10% of the dentists in the United States possess. Check out her website for free information on modern dental techniques. www.Akrondentalconcepts.com.

Being a woman in a predominantly male profession, Dr. Aldrich has learned how to play the game in the business world. She has learned how to use wit as well as psychology to dominate the field of dentistry. Now she wants to help other women who struggle with their inner demons, how not only to survive in the business world, but to work their way to the top! Dr. Aldrich uses the goal-setting skills that are in the book in her real life to plan her personal and professional steps.

"It's our right and duty to become successful in the world," states Dr. Aldrich. "But it's our *responsibility* as women to help others do the same!"

Other Books by Power Source Media, LLC

There's No Crying in the Man's World Home Study Course

This multimedia kit shows all women no matter what age, different ways to reach their "Perfect Day." Dr. Aldrich uses these principles in her own life to reach her goals each and every day.

This kit contains CD interviews from professional women that have made a difference in the workforce. Dr. Aldrich asks these women tough questions regarding how they've become successful, and she brings these tips to you. Included are tips on job interviews, resume building, communication skills, and much, much more.

This kit also contains a workbook that shows you in simple but great detail how to create a goal and then reach it. This is the same workbook that Dr. Aldrich uses to make tough decisions for both her dental practice and her thriving publishing company.

This is a great gift to give to a college student or a newly appointed corporate worker.

You can find this kit at www.thereisnocrying.com

If Your Walls Talked

This is a multimedia kit that shows the small business owner what different types of media can do for them in their internal marketing efforts.

Dr. Aldrich herself has these videos in her waiting room and in less than eight months they have been responsible for over $175,000 worth of unsolicited sales in her dental office. Dr. Aldrich and her marketing director Steven Reckner show you how she uses "social proof" to drive in herds of patients into her practice each and every day.

If Your Walls Talked teaches you how to use the well-known facts of marketing to sell more treatment! You learn how to use the psychology of the "buying" process to educate as well as create the emotional response that some patients need to proceed with treatment. *If Your Walls Talked* is a valuable resource for every service-oriented business. We will teach you how to use your successful finished treatment cases to sell more of them quicker and with less effort on your part. *If Your Walls Talked* will educate your patients on all of the procedures and specials that you are currently offering to your patients. *If Your Walls Talked* will take out the "salesmen" in your case presentation. It will "pre-qualify" your patients. Your patients will come in to see you ready to buy. They will ask you for treatment and take an active role in improving their health.

If Your Walls Talked will show you how to use all of those "before" and "after" photos that are collecting dust in your waiting room and actively use them to create a video that will make those dull, boring photos jump through the screen at your patients and educate them on what you can do for them.

If Your Walls Talked will show you the power of "social proof" and will allow you to use the space that you have but aren't using to advertise you and your services.

1. This kit contains DVD tutorials that teach the small business owner how to make a multi-media movie from a program that all pc's already

have! This movie can run in their main lobby or waiting room 24 hours a day, 7 days a week and will bring in hundreds if not thousands of dollars in sales to your business without you even giving your prospects your sales pitch!

2. This kit also contains a full color manual that shows the small business owner how to create "social proof." This "social proof" uses the resources that you already have in your office but aren't using. The manual shows what products are needed to make your customers become pre-qualified prospects that come to *you* for business.

You can check out this product on www.ifyourwallstalked.com.

Special Free Gift

Copy this page and fax it back to 330-666-7430

Test drive three months of Stephanie Aldrich's Newsletter called "The Power Approach"

Receive a steady stream of marketing and business building advice

Yes Stephanie, I want to take you up on your offer of a FREE three month subscription to your newsletter "The Power Approach" which includes:

1. Business building tips
2. Interviews with other powerful men and women that are making a difference in this world-for FREE
3. Access to product specials before the general public
4. Goal-setting advice with follow-up
5. "Ask Dr. Aldrich" teleseminars
6. And much, much more!

After the free three month subscription, you have no obligation to continue your subscription with us. If you wish to continue, your credit card will be charged a monthly fee of just $14.95. You can cancel at any time. Make a copy of this form, fill it out, and fax it to my office at 330-666-7430.

Name_____Email_____

Address_____

City/State/Zip_____Phone_____

Credit Card (circle) V MC # _____

Exp Date _____ Signature_____

Providing this information constitutes your permission for Power Source Media to contact you regarding related information via email, fax, and phone.

978-0-595-43341-4
0-595-43341-3

www.ingramcontent.com/pod-product-compliance
Lightning Source LLC
Chambersburg PA
CBHW021542200526
45163CB00014B/723